50 Walks in

WEST YORKSHIRE

First published 2001
Researched and written by John Morrison

Produced by AA Publishing
© Automobile Association Developments Limited 2001
Illustrations © Automobile Association Developments Limited 2001

Published by AA Publishing (a trading name of Automobile
Association Developments Limited, whose registered office is Norfolk
House, Priestley Road, Basingstoke, Hampshire RG24 9NY;
registered number 1878835)

ISBN 0 7495 2877 X

A CIP catalogue record for this book is available
from the British Library.

Visit the AA Publishing website at www.theAA.com

Paste-up and editorial by Outcrop Publishing Services
for AA Publishing

Colour reproduction by LC Repro
Printed in Italy by Rotolito Lombarda Spa

Legend

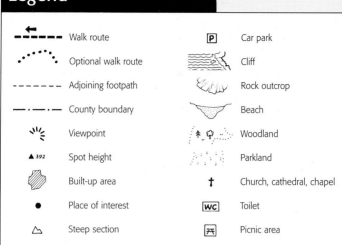

Walk route		P	Car park
Optional walk route			Cliff
Adjoining footpath			Rock outcrop
County boundary			Beach
Viewpoint			Woodland
▲ 392 Spot height			Parkland
Built-up area		†	Church, cathedral, chapel
● Place of interest		WC	Toilet
△ Steep section			Picnic area

West Yorkshire locator map

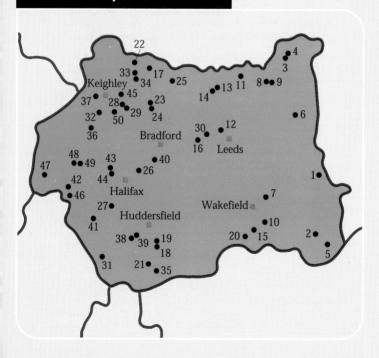

Contents

Contents

Rating: Each walk is rated for its relative difficulty compared to the other walks in this book. Walks marked 🚶🚶 🚶 🚶 are likely to be shorter and easier with little total ascent. The hardest walks are marked 🚶🚶 🚶🚶 🚶🚶 .

Walking in Safety: For advice and safety tips ➤ 128.

Introducing West Yorkshire

Everybody knows that Yorkshire has some special landscapes. Out in the Dales, the Moors, the Wolds and the Pennine hills, walkers can lengthen their stride, breathe fresh north country air and be alone with their thoughts. But what about West Yorkshire? That's Leeds and Bradford isn't it? Back-to-back houses, blackened mills, chip shops…

There's more than a little truth to most clichés. My adopted home town of Hebden Bridge is a case in point. If you had stood on any of the surrounding hills a hundred years ago, and gazed down into the valley, all you would have seen was the pall of smoke issuing from the chimneys of 33 textile mills. The town itself would have appeared just once each year: during the Wakes Week holiday, when the mills shut down.

Thankfully, life changes and here in West Yorkshire, it can change very quickly indeed. The textile trade went into terminal decline. The mills shut down forever. In a single generation Hebden Bridge changed from being a place that people wanted to leave, to a place that people want to visit. Having walked all over the north of England, I can confidently say that the countryside around Hebden Bridge offers walking every bit as good as the more celebrated Yorkshire Dales. I can lace up my boots, walk out of my front door and, within minutes, be tramping across the moors. And this close proximity of town and country is a pattern that's repeated all across West Yorkshire.

I make no apologies for favouring the west of the county a little more strongly than the east. To the west, where the Pennine hills create a natural barrier between the old foes of Yorkshire and Lancashire, is a truly wild landscape. This is where Pennine Way-farers get into their stride. Here are heather moors, riven by steep-sided wooded valleys known as 'cloughs'. Here are empty acres, sheep-cropped grass and the evocative cry of the curlew.

Local folk have a great fondness for the landscapes of West Yorkshire, and for a very good reason. The expansion of industry – and particularly the textile trades – forced a great many people off the land and into the towns. For generations the open spaces represented fresh air and freedom for those who laboured six days a week at the textile mills of Leeds, Bradford, Huddersfield, Batley and the other centres of industry strung along the valleys of the Rivers Colne, Aire and Calder. For those who value solitude, and the wide open spaces, try walks 31, 32, 34, 37, 41 and 42.

PUBLIC TRANSPORT ⓘ

West Yorkshire has an enviable public transport system. Most of these walks are within easy reach of frequent and relatively cheap buses and trains. For timetable information call Metroline on 0113 245 7676, or visit the website www.metro-wyorks.co.uk. You can also find bus and rail information on the internet at www.pti.org.uk.

The Pennine moors are rightly valued for their wild beauty. But we should also cherish the rural oases nearer to the West Yorkshire towns. Walks such as 5, 12, 15, 40 and 50 are valuable precisely because they are so close to centres of population. You will find beautiful deciduous woodlands, country parks, and the wildlife 'corridors' provided by canal tow paths and old railway lines.

Lovers of wildlife have a wide choice of walks. The Pennine moors are home to birds such as red grouse, kestrels and ring ouzels; the fast flowing rivers support dippers and wagtails. But if you want to see rare birds you should head to the east of the county where opencast coal mines have 'gone back to nature' as lakes and wetlands. Walks 1, 5, 7 and 10 visit some of the most interesting sites.

There's such diversity in the area that you can found yourself in quite unfamiliar surroundings, even close to places you may know very well. Take time to explore this rich county on foot and you will be thrilled at what you find to shatter the myths and preconceptions.

Using this Book

Information panels
An information panel for each walk shows its relative difficulty (▶ 5), the distance and total amount of ascent. An indication of the gradients you will encounter is shown by the rating ▲▲ ▲▲ ▲▲ (no steep slopes) to ▲▲ ▲▲ ▲▲ (several very steep slopes).

Maps
There are 30 maps, covering 40 of the walks. Some walks have a suggested option in the same area. The information panel for these walks will tell you how much extra walking is involved. On short-cut suggestions the panel will tell you the total distance if you set out from the start of the main walk. Where an option returns to the same point on the main walk, just the distance of the loop is given. Where an option leaves the main walk at one point and returns to it at another, then the distance shown is for the whole walk. The minimum time suggested is for reasonably fit walkers and doesn't allow for stops. Each walk has a suggested map. Laminated aqua3 maps are longer lasting and water resistant.

Start Points
The start of each walk is given as a six-figure grid reference prefixed by two letters indicating which 100km square of the National Grid it refers to. You'll find more information on grid references on most Ordnance Survey maps.

Dogs
We have tried to give dog owners useful advice about how dog friendly each walk is. Please respect other countryside users. Keep your dog under control, especially around livestock, and obey local bylaws and other dog control notices.

Car Parking
Many of the car parks suggested are public, but occasionally you may find you have to park on the roadside or in a lay-by. Please be considerate when you leave your car, ensuring that access roads or gates are not blocked and that other vehicles can pass safely.

Fairburn Ings and Ledsham

A visit to West Yorkshire's very own 'Lake District', now a bird reserve of national importance.

•DISTANCE•	5 miles (8km)
•MINIMUM TIME•	2hrs 30min
•ASCENT / GRADIENT•	131ft (40m) ▲▲▲
•LEVEL OF DIFFICULTY•	👫 👫 👫
•PATHS•	Good paths and tracks (some newly-created from spoil heaps), 7 stiles
•LANDSCAPE•	Lakes, riverside and reclaimed colliery spoil heaps
•SUGGESTED MAP•	aqua3 OS Explorer 289 Leeds
•START / FINISH•	Grid reference: SE 472278
•DOG FRIENDLINESS•	Keep on lead around main lake, due to wildfowl
•PARKING•	Free parking in Cut Road, Fairburn. From A1, drive into village, turn left 100yds (91m) past Three Horseshoes pub,
•PUBLIC TOILETS•	Fairburn Ings visitor centre

BACKGROUND TO THE WALK

The coalfields of West Yorkshire were most concentrated in the borough of Wakefield. Towns and villages grew up around the mines, and came to represent the epitome of northern industrial life. Mining was always a dangerous and dirty occupation, and it changed the landscape dramatically. Opencast mines swallowed up huge tracts of land, and the extensive spoil heaps were all-too-visible evidence of industry.

For the men of these communities, mining was almost the only work available. So when the industry went into decline, these communities were hit especially hard. Historians will look back at the mining industry and be amazed at the speed of this decline. Mines that were earmarked for expansion could be closed down a year or two later. To politicians of the left, the miners were sacrificial lambs; to those of the right, the miners exerted too much power. For good or ill the mining industry was decimated, and thousands of miners lost their livelihoods.

The death of the industry was emphasised by the closing down of Caphouse Colliery and its subsequent conversion into the National Coal Mining Museum for England (► 55). The spoil heaps that scarred the landscape are going back to nature, a process hastened by tree planting and other reclamation schemes. Opencast workings are being transformed into lakes and wetlands – valuable havens for wildfowl and migrating birds. Within a single generation West and South Yorkshire may have a network of lakes to rival the Norfolk Broads. In the meantime, these industrial wastelands are still rather scruffy. Not that the birds seem to mind...

Fairburn Ings Nature Reserve

Fairburn Ings, now under the stewardship of the Royal Society for the Protection of Birds (RSPB), was one of the earliest examples of colliery reclamation – being designated a Local Nature Reserve in 1957. The result is arguably the most important nature reserve in West Yorkshire. The site seems rather unpromising; it's hemmed in by the A1, the conurbation of

Castleford, the River Aire, a railway and old spoil heaps. Nevertheless, the stark outlines of the spoil heaps are now softened by banks of silver birches, and mining subsidence has created a broad expanse of water near the village of Fairburn, as well as smaller pools and flashes.

There are plenty of birds to be seen at all times of the year, though the numbers of ducks, geese, swans and gulls are at their highest during the winter months. The 600 acres (243ha) of wetlands are a magnet for birds during the spring and autumn migration. In summer there are many species of wildlife nesting on the scrapes and islands – including terns and a large, noisy colony of black-headed gulls. The best places from which to view all this activity are the public hides that overlook the lake.

Ledsham

Hidden away from the traffic hammering up and down the nearby A1, the estate village of Ledsham is a tranquil little backwater. Behind the Saxon church – one of the oldest in West Yorkshire – is a row of picturesque almshouses. The Chequers Inn is an old and characterful country pub with, unusually, a six-day licence. Some 170 years ago, so the story goes, the one-time lady of the manor was on her way to church, when she saw some of her farm-hands in a drunken state. To avoid this happening in future, she decreed that Sundays in Ledsham should be 'dry'.

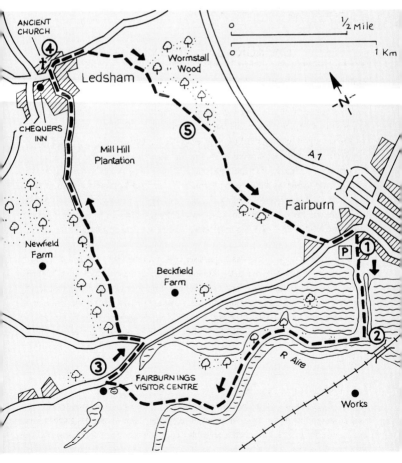

Walk 1

Walk 1 Directions

① Walk down **Cut Road** as it narrows to a track. Soon you have the main lake to your right, and a smaller stretch of water to your left. When the track forks, keep right (unless you want to visit the first of the bird hides, in which case detour to the left). The path finishes at the end of the lake, on approaching the **River Aire**.

WHERE TO EAT AND DRINK ⓘ

The **Chequers Inn** in Ledsham harks back to the past in more ways than one. The exposed beams and open fires give the pub a homely atmosphere. Excellent food makes the place popular for lunches with walkers and locals. Closed on Sundays.

---

② Go right here, to join a path along the top of a ridge (actually an old spoil heap), with the river to your left and the lake right. Look out for a couple of other bird hides, before you lose sight of the lake. The path crosses a broader expanse of spoil heap, through scrubland, following the river in a broad arc to the right, before descending to a stile above another small mere. Bear right on a broad track and drop down into the car park of the **Fairburn Ings visitor centre**.

WHILE YOU'RE THERE ⓘ

There's a mixture of old and new at **Ferrybridge**, where the M62 crosses the A1. When travellers from the south and east reach this point, and see the huge cooling towers of Ferrybridge Power Station, they know they have arrived in West Yorkshire. But adjacent to the motorway bridge is a surprising anachronism: an 18th-century bridge by the Yorkshire architect John Carr, better known for his work on Harewood House.

---

③ Meet a road. Go right for 100yds (91m), then go left (signed '**Ledston and Kippax**') for just 100yds (91m), and pick up a path on your right that hugs the right-hand fringe of a wood. Beyond the wood, take a path between fields; it broadens to a track as you approach the village of **Ledsham**. At a new estate of houses, turn right, along **Manor Garth**.

④ You arrive in the village by the ancient church. Walk right, along the road (or, for refreshments, go left to the **Chequers Inn**). Beyond the village, where the road bears left, take a gate on the right, giving access to a good track uphill. Where the main track goes right, into fields, continue along a track ahead, into woodland. Leave the wood by a stile, crossing pasture on a grassy track. Two stiles take you across a narrow spur of woodland.

⑤ Head slightly left, uphill, across the next field, to follow a fence and hedgerow. Continue – soon on a better track – across a stile. Beyond the next stile the track bears left, towards farm buildings: but you keep straight on, with a fence on your right, along the field path. Through a metal gate, join an access track downhill. Go left, when you meet the road, and back into the village of **Fairburn**.

WHAT TO LOOK FOR

Be sure to take a pair of binoculars with you. Fairburn Ings is a bird reserve of national importance and, especially during the spring and autumn migrations, all kinds of rare birds can be seen. There are a number of strategically sited hides along this walk, from which you can watch the birds without disturbing them. Watch especially for the rare but inconspicuous gadwall, pochard and golden plover.

High Ackworth and East Hardwick

An undemanding stroll through history in rolling, pastoral countryside to the east of Wakefield.

•DISTANCE•	5 miles (8km)
•MINIMUM TIME•	2hrs 30min
•ASCENT / GRADIENT•	131ft (40m) ▲ ▲ ▲
•LEVEL OF DIFFICULTY•	秧 秧 秧
•PATHS•	Mostly field paths; care should be taken with route finding, on the first section to East Hardwick, 11 stiles
•LANDSCAPE•	Gently rolling, arable country
•SUGGESTED MAP•	aqua3 OS Explorer 278 Sheffield & Barnsley
•START / FINISH•	Grid reference: SE 441180
•DOG FRIENDLINESS•	Dogs on leads in villages and through farmyards
•PARKING•	A few parking places in middle of High Ackworth, near church and village green
•PUBLIC TOILETS•	None on route

BACKGROUND TO THE WALK

With its village green acting as the centrepiece for some fine old houses, High Ackworth has a pleasantly old-fashioned air and is now designated a conservation area. Today the village is best known for its school, founded by a prominent Quaker, John Fothergil, to teach the children of 'Friends not in affluence'. Ackworth Quaker School opened its doors on October 18, 1779, a day still commemorated by the pupils as Founder's Day. Opposite the village green are almshouses, built in 1741 to house 'a schoolmaster and six poor women'. Nearby Ackworth Old Hall, dating from the early 17th century, is supposed to be haunted by John Nevison, a notorious robber and highwayman. His most famous act of daring was in 1676 when he rode from Rochester to York in just 15 hours. The story goes that he committed a robbery and then was afraid his victim might have recognised him. Fleeing the scene, he put the 230 miles (373km) behind him in record time. On his arrival in York, was seen asking the Lord Mayor the time. After his arrest he used the Mayor as his alibi and he was acquitted. No one believed the journey could be made in so short a time. The feat is often wrongly attributed to another highwayman, Dick Turpin, who was not yet born.

Plague Story

Until the Reformation, the stone plinth on the village green was topped by a cross. It was knocked off by Cromwell's troops, whose puritanical dislike of religious ornament led them to destroy the church font too. The cross had been erected in memory of Father Thomas Balne of nearby Nostell Priory, who once preached from here. During a pilgrimage to Rome, he succumbed to the plague. When his body was being brought back to the priory, mourners insisted on opening the coffin here in High Ackworth. As a result, the plague was inflicted upon the community, with devastating results. The Plague Stone, by the Pontefract Road, dates from a second devastating outbreak in 1645 (► While You're There).

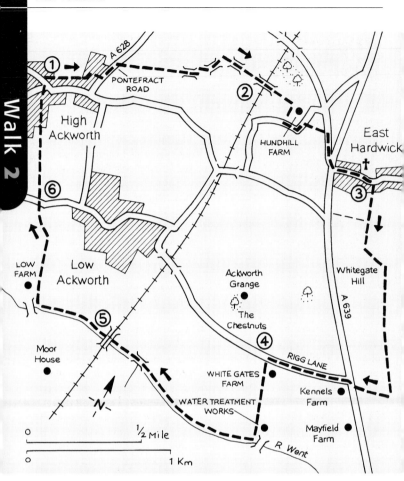

Walk 2 Directions

① From the top of the village green, take a narrow ginnel immediately to the right of **Manor House**. Beyond a stile made of stone slabs (not the last you'll see today), keep to the right-hand edge of a small field, to another stile. A ginnel brings you out into **Woodland Grove**; go left here, then first right, to meet the A628, **Pontefract Road**. Go left, but for just 100yds (91m). Look out on the right for a gap in the hedgerow and a footpath sign (opposite a house called **Tall Trees**). Walk straight across a field (follow the direction of the sign), to a tiny footbridge over a beck. Continue along the right-hand edge of the next field, over another tiny bridge. Keep ahead between fields – going sharp left, then sharp right, over another footbridge – to follow a hedgerow. When you come to a gap in the hedge, head straight across the next two fields (towards the houses you see ahead).

② Take a bridge over a railway line, and continue between fields towards **Hundhill Farm**. Keep right at the farm's boundary wall, to a stile. Bear left along the lane; after

WHAT TO LOOK FOR ⓘ

Village greens are uncommon features in West Yorkshire, a county in which even the smallest community can feel like a town. But the Industrial Revolution passed Ackworth by; no mill chimneys ever disturbed the symmetry. Surrounded by buildings of character – including the parish church, Manor House and a row of almshouses – Ackworth has managed to retain its village atmosphere.

just 75yds (68m), and after a left-hand bend, take a gap stile in the wall on your right, on to an enclosed path. Beyond the next stile, bear right along a minor road that soon meets the A639. Cross the road, passing the old village pump, and walk into the village of **East Hardwick**. Beyond the church, where the road bears left, look out for a sign ('Public Bridleway') on your right, just before a house called **Bridleways**.

③ Go right here, along a track between hedgerows. Soon after the track goes left, take a gap in the hedge to your right. Follow a field path uphill, keeping a hedgerow to your right. At the top of this narrow field, keep straight ahead on a footpath between fields. Follow a drainage channel to meet a crossing track. Go right here, to cross over the A639 again. Take the road ahead (this is **Rigg Lane**) and, at **White Gates Farm**, go left, between farm buildings, on to a concrete track.

④ Follow this track past a water treatment works, to a concrete bridge over the **River Went** (notice the old packhorse bridge next to it). Without crossing either bridge, bear right, on a field-edge path, to accompany the river. A little plank bridge takes you across a side-beck, before you walk beneath the six arches of a railway viaduct.

⑤ Continue by the riverside, passing (not crossing) a stone bridge over the river. Bear right here, across the corner of a field, in front of the barns of **Low Farm**, to join a field-edge path. Follow a hedge towards houses, to a stile and a road. This is **Low Ackworth**.

⑥ Cross the road and take a ginnel between houses. Beyond a stile at the far end, bear half left across a field to a stile and across another field. A stile gives access to another ginnel. Continue along **Hill Drive**, soon bearing right, down into a cul-de-sac. At the bottom, take a narrow ginnel on the left, to arrive back in **High Ackworth** near the village green.

WHERE TO EAT AND DRINK ⓘ

The **Brown Cow** is pleasantly situated on Pontefract Road in the middle of High Ackworth, overlooking the village green. There are benches out front and it's open all day. They serve a range of bar meals between noon and 2PM and on Thursday and Friday evenings.

WHILE YOU'RE THERE ⓘ

The **Plague Stone** stands outside Ackworth, at the junction of the A628 Pontefract Road and Sandy Gate Lane. It is an evocative relic of when the Black Death swept through these communities, in 1645, killing over 150 villagers. The hollow in the stone would have been filled with vinegar to disinfect coins left in payment for food brought from outside the village while it was in quarantine. The victims are thought to have been buried in the 'Burial Field' a few hundred paces to the east. Only the year before the same fields had witnessed some bloody skirmishing between the Parliamentarian troops and Royalists and may well have already been used for mass burials.

Wetherby and the River Wharfe

Around a handsome country market town and along a stretch of the mature River Wharfe.

•DISTANCE•	3½ miles (5.7km)
•MINIMUM TIME•	2hrs
•ASCENT / GRADIENT•	65ft (20m) ▲ ▲ ▲
•LEVEL OF DIFFICULTY•	𝓀 𝓀 𝓀
•PATHS•	Field paths and good tracks, a little road-walking, 1 stile
•LANDSCAPE•	Arable land, mostly on the flat
•SUGGESTED MAP•	aqua3 OS Outdoor Leisure 289 Leeds
•START / FINISH•	Grid reference: SE 405479
•DOG FRIENDLINESS•	No particular problems
•PARKING•	Free car parking in Wilderness car park, close to river, just over bridge as you drive into Wetherby from south
•PUBLIC TOILETS•	Wetherby

BACKGROUND TO THE WALK

Wetherby, at the north east corner of the county, is not your typical West Yorkshire town. Most of the houses are built of pale stone, topped with roofs of red tiles – a type of architecture more usually found in North Yorkshire. With its riverside developments and air of prosperity, the Wetherby of today is a favoured place to live. The flat, arable landscape, too, is very different to Pennine Yorkshire. Here, on the fringes of the Vale of York, the soil is rich and dark and productive – the fields divided up by fences and hedgerows rather than dry-stone walls.

Historic Town

The town has a long history. A brief glance at an Ordnance Survey map reveals that Wetherby grew up around a tight curve in the River Wharfe. Its importance as a river crossing was recognised by the building of a castle, possibly in the 12th century, of which only the foundations remain. The first mention of a bridge was in 1233. A few years later, in 1240, the Knights Templar were granted a royal charter to hold a market in Wetherby.

At Flint Mill, visited on this walk, flints were ground for use in the pottery industry of Leeds. The town also had two corn mills, powered by water from the River Wharfe. The distinctive – and recently restored – weir helped to maintain a good head of water to turn the waterwheels. In general though, the Industrial Revolution made very little impression on Wetherby.

The town grew in importance not from what it made, but from where it was situated. In the days of coach travel, the 400-mile (648km) trip between London and Edinburgh was quite an ordeal for passengers and horses alike. And Wetherby, at the half-way point of the journey, became a convenient stop for mail and passenger coaches. The trade was busiest during the second half of the 18th century, when the town had upwards of 40 inns and alehouses. Coaching inns such as the Swan, the Talbot and the Angel catered for weary

Walk 3

travellers and provided stabling for the horses. The Angel was known as 'the Halfway House' and had stables for more than a hundred horses. The Great North Road ran across the town's splendid arched bridge, and right through the middle of the town. With coaches arriving and departing daily, it must have presented a busy scene

When the railway arrived in the 1840s, Wetherby's role as a staging post went into decline. The Great North Road was eventually re-routed – to skirt around the town, rather than run straight through the centre. Even the name was lost, with the road now being known, more prosaically, as the A1. When Dr Beeching wielded his axe in 1964, Wetherby lost its railway too. Ironically, a town that had once been synonymous with coach travel is now a peaceful backwater, re-inventing itself once again as an upmarket commuter town. The area around the River Wharfe is being renovated, to provide riverside apartments, pleasant walks and picnic sites. These days most people will probably know the town from listening to the racing results.

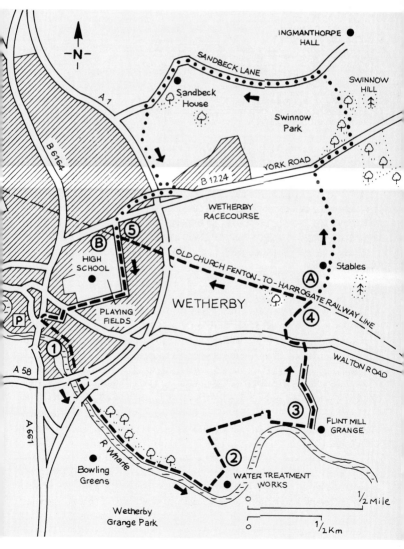

Walk 3

Walk 3 Directions

① Walk to the far end of the car park, to follow a path with the **River Wharfe** on the right and cliffs to the left. You pass in quick succession beneath the shallow arches of two modern bridges, carrying the A58 and A1 roads across the **Wharfe**. Go through a kissing gate to continue on a riverside path, soon with open fields on your left. Take another kissing gate to arrive at Wetherby's **water treatment works**.

② Go left here, up a track around the perimeter fence. After 150yds (138m) you meet a metalled track at the works' main entrance; go left here. At the top of an incline, where the track bears slightly to the right, you have a choice of routes. Your path is sharp right, along a grassy track between fields. You soon approach the wooded slope that overlooks the **River Wharfe**. Take a stile, and follow the line of trees to a farm, **Flint Mill Grange**. Enter the farmyard and take the farm access road to the left.

WHILE YOU'RE THERE
Wetherby's nearest neighbour is **Boston Spa** which, like Ilkley, became a prosperous spa town on the River Wharfe. It was the accidental discovery, in 1744, of a mineral spring that changed the town's fortunes. The salty taste and sulphurous smell were enough to convince people that the spring water had health-giving properties, and a pump room and bath house were built to cater for well-heeled visitors. The town's great days as a spa town are over but, with some splendid Georgian buildings, it has retained an air of elegance.

③ Meet **Walton Road** and walk left for 75yds (68m); then go right, along a metalled drive (this is signed as both a bridleway and the entrance to **Wetherby Racecourse**). After a gate you have a choice of routes, bear left here, downhill, to join the trackbed of the old Church Fenton-to-Harrogate railway line, which carried its last train in 1964. This is Point Ⓐ, where the longer Walk 4 diverges.

WHERE TO EAT AND DRINK
As a market town, and a staging post on the Great North Road, Wetherby is well provided with a choice of pubs, cafés and old coaching inns. The **Angel** on the High Street serves traditional bar meals at very reasonable prices and has good facilities for children. It's open all day, as is the nearby **Red Lion,** which also serves a range of good food.

④ Go left, to enjoy level walking along the railway trackbed, until you approach the A1 road, raised up on an embankment as it skirts around Wetherby. Take the underpass beneath the road, and bear right along **Freemans Way**, until you meet **Hallfield Lane**, (Point Ⓑ on Walk 4).

⑤ Walk left, along **Hallfield Lane**, which bears right around the playing fields of **Wetherby High School** and back into the centre of **Wetherby**.

WHAT TO LOOK FOR
Unlike many towns in West Yorkshire, Wetherby still holds its general market every Thursday, with the stalls arranged around the handsome little town hall. Nearby are the Shambles, a row of collonaded stalls built in 1811 to house a dozen butchers' shops.

A Day at the Races

Extend the walk with a circuit of Wetherby's famous racecourse.
See map and information panel for Walk 3

•DISTANCE•	5½ miles (8.8km)
•MINIMUM TIME•	3hrs
•ASCENT / GRADIENT•	82ft (25m) ▲ ▲ ▲
•LEVEL OF DIFFICULTY•	👫 👫 👫

Walk 4 Directions (Walk 3 option)

The flat landscape around Wetherby lent itself to arable and dairy farming, while horse racing was a popular pursuit on nearby Clifford Moor by the 17th century. But racing didn't find a permanent home at Wetherby until 1891, when a course was laid out on land belonging to the Montagu family of nearby Ingmanthorpe Hall. In 1929 a railway station was built alongside the racecourse.

Of the nine racecourses in Yorkshire, Wetherby is the only one devoted entirely to racing over jumps, attracting the best steeplechasers from all over the country. It stages top quality National Hunt race days between October and May, as well as a perennially popular two-day meeting at Christmas.

At Point Ⓐ, continue along the metalled drive, ignoring turn-offs into the car parks of **Wetherby Racecourse**. Pass the new Millennium Stand; keep following the road, and the exit signs, past the eastern end of the racecourse itself to meet **York Road**. Go right, along the road, for 200yds (182m), then bear left along a metalled drive signed to **Swinnow Hill**. Where the track bears slightly to the right, towards the house, you go left, through a gate, on to a field-edge path – with the field to your left and a spur of woodland to your right. Soon you come to a good track; this is **Sandbeck Lane** (and the imposing house to the right is **Ingmanthorpe Hall**).

Bear left, along this track; when it forks, keep straight ahead on a rougher track, with a hedgerow to your right. The track meanders pleasantly between large fields of rich brown soil. When the main track goes right, keep ahead, on a grassy track between hedgerows. Pass a couple of houses, as the track improves. Immediately before a bungalow (with stables attached), go left on to a field-edge path, slightly uphill. You soon join a metalled lane, now having only a thorny hedge between you and bustling traffic on the A1. The lane soon bears left, away from the A1. After 100yds (91m), in front of houses, the lane forks. Go right here, to the York road. Bear right, along this road, to cross the A1. After 300yds (274m), turn left down **Hallfield Lane**, rejoining Walk 3 at Point Ⓑ.

Upton's Reclaimed Country

From the scars of Upton coal mine, a nature reserve is created.

•DISTANCE•	3 miles (4.8km)
•MINIMUM TIME•	1hr 30min
•ASCENT / GRADIENT•	65ft (20m)
•LEVEL OF DIFFICULTY•	
•PATHS•	Disused railway line and good tracks, no stiles
•LANDSCAPE•	Reclaimed colliery land
•SUGGESTED MAP•	aqua3 OS Explorer 278 Sheffield & Barnsley
•START / FINISH•	Grid reference: SE 478133
•DOG FRIENDLINESS•	No particular problems
•PARKING•	Car park on Waggon Lane, Upton, next to fishing lake
•PUBLIC TOILETS•	None on route

Walk 5 Directions

The scenery of the south-eastern corner of West Yorkshire, including the borough of Wakefield, contrasts markedly with the moorlands to the west. The landscape has undergone many changes in recent years, mostly due to the rise – and decline – of coal mining. But the effects have not been all-embracing. The villages of North Elmsall and South Elmsall, for example, have had very different histories. When Frickley Colliery opened in 1903, it transformed South Elmsall into a bustling town, leaving North Elmsall as the quiet backwater it still is today.

With the benefit of perspective, historians will look back on Yorkshire's coal industry as a brief period in the county's history. The remains of primitive mines, just

shallow 'bell pits', can be found all around the county, but only in a few places were the coal deposits sufficiently extensive or accessible to make mining profitable for the early miner. The second phase of the Industrial Revolution – when the mills were converted from water- to steam-power – provided a huge financial spur. The Yorkshire coalfields now had the markets to make investment in deep-mined coal worthwhile. They became famous throughout the world, but there was a heavy price to pay. Long hours, dangerous working conditions and an explosive atmosphere was the miners' lot.

After the closure of the collieries, and the inevitable human and environmental deprivation that followed, it's gratifying to see these areas being given a new lease of life. Unsightly pits are being re-developed into lakes for wildfowl, insectlife and fishing. Disused railway lines are being transformed into footpaths and valuable new cycle routes. New industries too, are bringing life back to the local

---

WHERE TO EAT AND DRINK ⓘ

The **Upton Arms**, on Upton High Street, is conveniently placed for refreshments, near the start of this walk.

Walk 5

economy, and the bare colliery spoil heaps have been changed beyond all recognition as, replanted and grassed over, they have emerged as a valuable wildlife and leisure resource for the local communities.

This walk begins at the fishing lake created on land once occupied by the Upton colliery, sunk in 1924 but closed in 1966. It continues along the trackbed of the old Hull-to-Barnsley railway, which was another line lost to the Beeching axe, back in the 1960s. You pass the remains of **Upton Station**. The old railway is now a broad corridor for both wildlife and recreation. During the summer months there are songbirds and butterflies aplenty. At the half way point of the walk is **Johnny Brown's Common**, another area much altered, where a lake offers refuge to wildfowl.

To the left of the fishing lake is an access gate. Walk to the right, past the lake, to meet a broad cinder track: this is the trackbed of the old Hull-to-Barnsley railway. Follow the track, to the right, passing a small pond and then the platform of a long-abandoned railway station. There are a number of side tracks; just keep to the straight, obvious track and you won't go wrong. Beyond a gate you will reach a roundabout on the A638. Walk left, around the roundabout, to locate another metal gate. A footpath leads

downhill to rejoin the route of the railway trackbed. Soon your track is raised above the level of the surrounding fields. When the colour of the track turns from grey cinders to white, you may want to detour down to your right, on a path that leads to two more secluded ponds. Otherwise carry straight on, along the track. Follow a fence on the left, gradually uphill. Continue to follow the fence as it bears left at the top of the hill, to join a broad track descending to a larger lake, with three islands.

Keep to the left-hand side of the lake, on the track (unless you want to take the path around the lake). Turn left, at the far end of the lake, to follow a fence. The track bends first left, then right, to run parallel to the railway line you walked earlier. Follow this track to meet a road. Cross the road, and take the lane opposite.

Cross the A638, continuing in the same direction into the little village of **North Elmsall**. As the road goes left, past the church, take a step stile in the wall on the left (signed '**footpath to Upton**'). Walk straight across one field, then another, pass a little pond and reach the railway trackbed once again. Go right here soon taking a path, left, to arrive back at the car park in **Upton**.

Walk 6

The Kingdom of Elmet

A walk from Barwick in Elmet – boasting the country's tallest maypole.

•DISTANCE•	8 miles (12.9km)
•MINIMUM TIME•	4hrs
•ASCENT / GRADIENT•	130ft (40m)
•LEVEL OF DIFFICULTY•	
•PATHS•	Field paths; good track through Parlington Estate, 3 stiles
•LANDSCAPE•	Arable, parkland, woods
•SUGGESTED MAP•	aqua3 OS Explorer 289 Leeds
•START / FINISH•	Grid reference: SE 399374
•DOG FRIENDLINESS•	Keep on lead through villages
•PARKING•	Roadside parking in Barwick in Elmet, near maypole
•PUBLIC TOILETS•	None on route

BACKGROUND TO THE WALK

Elmet was one of a number of small independent British kingdoms to emerge during the so-called Dark Ages, between the end of Roman rule and the conquering of southern Britain, in AD 560, by the Saxon King Edwin. At the height of its powers the kingdom included most of present-day West Yorkshire, and extended from the River Humber in the east, to the Pennine hills in the west. Whilst it is known that Elmet was a realm of some importance, there is little solid archaeological evidence for its existence, apart from a series of defensive earthworks.

Barwick in Elmet
For such a small town, Barwick in Elmet has an air of self-importance. And with good reason: this is one of West Yorkshire's most ancient settlements. Before the Roman invasion it was a town of some size, and after the Romans had left the area it became the capital of the local kingdom of Elmet. A road, 'The Boyle', bends around the castle mound: here was a 12th-century Norman fortification, built on the site of an Iron Age hill fort.

Barwick boasts the tallest maypole in the country. Every three years it is taken down, given a new coat of paint and hoisted back up to its full height again. It's a job for which a lot of local labour is required, armed with ropes, ladders and pitchforks.

Aberford
The road that runs through Aberford is of Roman origin, built around AD 70. On an Ordnance Survey map you can trace its ruler-straight orientation from Aberford down to Castleford. Even the name survives on the map: Roman Ridge Road. Aberford was once an important stopping point for travellers up and down the Great North Road. There were coaching inns on the roadside where horses and passengers could be fed and watered.

Black Horse Farm, to the north of the town, was once the Black Horse Inn, a favourite haunt of John Nevison, a famous local highwayman. When he rode from London to York in a single day (▶ 11), he changed horses at the Black Horse. The great road of today, better known as the A1(M), makes the smallest of detours, around the town, to allow the juggernauts to hurry past at speed. This leaves Aberford free from the roar of traffic.

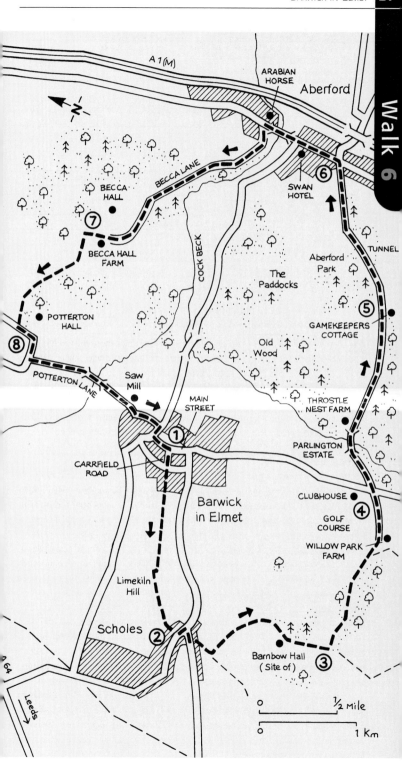

Walk 6

Walk 6 Directions

① Walk south along **Main Street**, from the maypole in the direction of **Scholes**. After 150yds (138m) turn right into **Carrfield Road**. Where the metalled road ends, continue straight ahead on a track, which soon becomes a field-edge path. From here, to the outskirts of **Scholes**, you keep straight ahead across fields. The route is easy to find, following a hedgerow (first on your right, then on your left, then on your right again) to meet a road.

WHAT TO LOOK FOR ⓘ

On the opposite side of the A1 from Aberford, just off the B1217, is **Lead Church**, all alone in the middle of a field. Lead is one of Yorkshire's 'lost' villages. All that's left of a once thriving community is this delectable 14th-century church and nearby Lead Hall Farm.

---

② Bear left for 100yds (91m) to take a road to the right, signed to **Leeds**. Cross this road and take a stony bridleway ahead, soon leaving **Scholes** behind. At a junction of tracks, keep left, on the most obvious track. When another track comes in from the left you cross a barrier. As you approach a larger wood, leave the track and go left, on a track fringing the woodland.

③ Through a gate you skirt a golf course. Keep right where the path forks, crossing two fairways, to a track that soon passes **Willow Park Farm**. Keep straight ahead to meet a road by the golfers' clubhouse.

④ Cross the road and continue on a farm track into the **Parlington Estate**. Pass to the right of **Throstle Nest Farm**, with fields to your left and woodland on your right.

At **Gamekeepers Cottage**, a curious-looking house with a wall around it, your path diverges.

⑤ Keep straight ahead on a path through woodland. Bear right, just before a tunnel, to avoid walking through the gloom. The path rejoins your original route at the far end of the tunnel. Pass a gatehouse to arrive in the village of **Aberford**.

⑥ Walk left, along the road, passing the **Swan Hotel**, the bridge over **Cock Beck** and a pub named, uniquely, the **Arabian Horse**. Go left, opposite this pub, along **Becca Lane**, keeping left when it forks. Beyond a gatehouse follow a sandy track towards **Becca Hall**. 300yds (274m) before the hall, bear left, on a grassy track, keeping to a fence on your left. Pass **Becca Hall Farm**.

⑦ Continue ahead on the farm track for 100yds (91m) to a post with a yellow diamond on it. Bear left here, downhill, to cross a field; there is no discernible path. Pass another waymarker post and walk across the next field (aim for the solitary tree). At the top of the field follow the field-edge, to a stile. Follow another path skirting woods on your left. At the next stile, by a gate, bear half-right across a field, to a stile, and meet a road.

⑧ Walk left, along the road. It bears sharp right at an entrance to **Potterton Hall**; go left down **Potterton Lane** back into **Barwick in Elmet**.

WHERE TO EAT AND DRINK ⓘ

The **Gascoigne Arms** is a very old pub in the centre of the village, close to the maypole. The **Arabian Horse** – at the half-way point of the walk, in Aberford – is another good place to have lunch.

Walk 7

Navigating From Stanley Ferry

An exploration of the River Calder and the Aire and Calder Navigation.

•DISTANCE•	6 miles (9.7km)
•MINIMUM TIME•	3hrs
•ASCENT / GRADIENT•	82ft (25m) ▲ ▲ ▲
•LEVEL OF DIFFICULTY•	👫 👫 👫
•PATHS•	Canal tow path and other good paths, no stiles
•LANDSCAPE•	Flat land and reclaimed colliery works
•SUGGESTED MAP•	aqua3 OS Explorer 289 Leeds
•START / FINISH•	Grid reference: SE 355229
•DOG FRIENDLINESS•	Can be off lead on tow path
•PARKING•	Large car park at Stanley Ferry Marina
•PUBLIC TOILETS•	At marina

BACKGROUND TO THE WALK

The Yorkshire coal mines developed during medieval times. As productive as the coal seams were, the industry was held back by the high costs of transport. The same problem faced the woollen industry. Only very small craft could carry cloth along the Aire to Goole and Hull, where it was transferred to ships bound for European markets.

The Aire and Calder Navigation

The River Calder meandered circuitously through the flat landscape to the east of Wakefield. In 1699 William III authorised the Aire and Calder rivers to be made navigable to the tidal Ouse. Leeds and Wakefield wool merchants paid for the canalising and deepening of parts of the rivers. The Aire and Calder Navigation took a more direct route, with comparatively few locks, so both costs and journey times were cut significantly. The first large vessels reached Leeds Bridge in 1700 and Wakefield the following year. The Aire and Calder Navigation proved to be a profitable investment for all concerned and continued to be upgraded to allow ever larger vessels to negotiate the locks. Unlike most other canals, it is still used for commercial traffic. With the decline of the Yorkshire coal industry, however, the loads are mostly bulk deliveries of sand and gravel.

There are two aqueducts, side by side, at Stanley Ferry. The older aqueduct, built between 1836 and 1839 for the Aire and Calder Navigation Company, is believed to have been the first iron suspension bridge in the world. It's an impressive structure, carrying the canal across the River Calder in a cast iron trough, suspended from cast iron arches. The new aqueduct, a more prosaic concrete structure, dates from 1981.

About 1860 a new system was invented for bulk transportation of coal by canal. Floating tubs, each one capable of holding up to 10 tons of coal, were linked together and pulled by steam tugs. Having reached the port, these tubs were lifted out of the water by primitive hoists and their contents swiftly emptied into ships' holds. This idea was refined by hauliers on the Aire and Calder Navigation, who developed tubs capable of carrying 40 tons of coal, and hydraulic machines for loading and unloading them. These tubs became known, affectionately, as Tom Puddings. They were a common sight on the waterway, with as many as 30 joined together in a line.

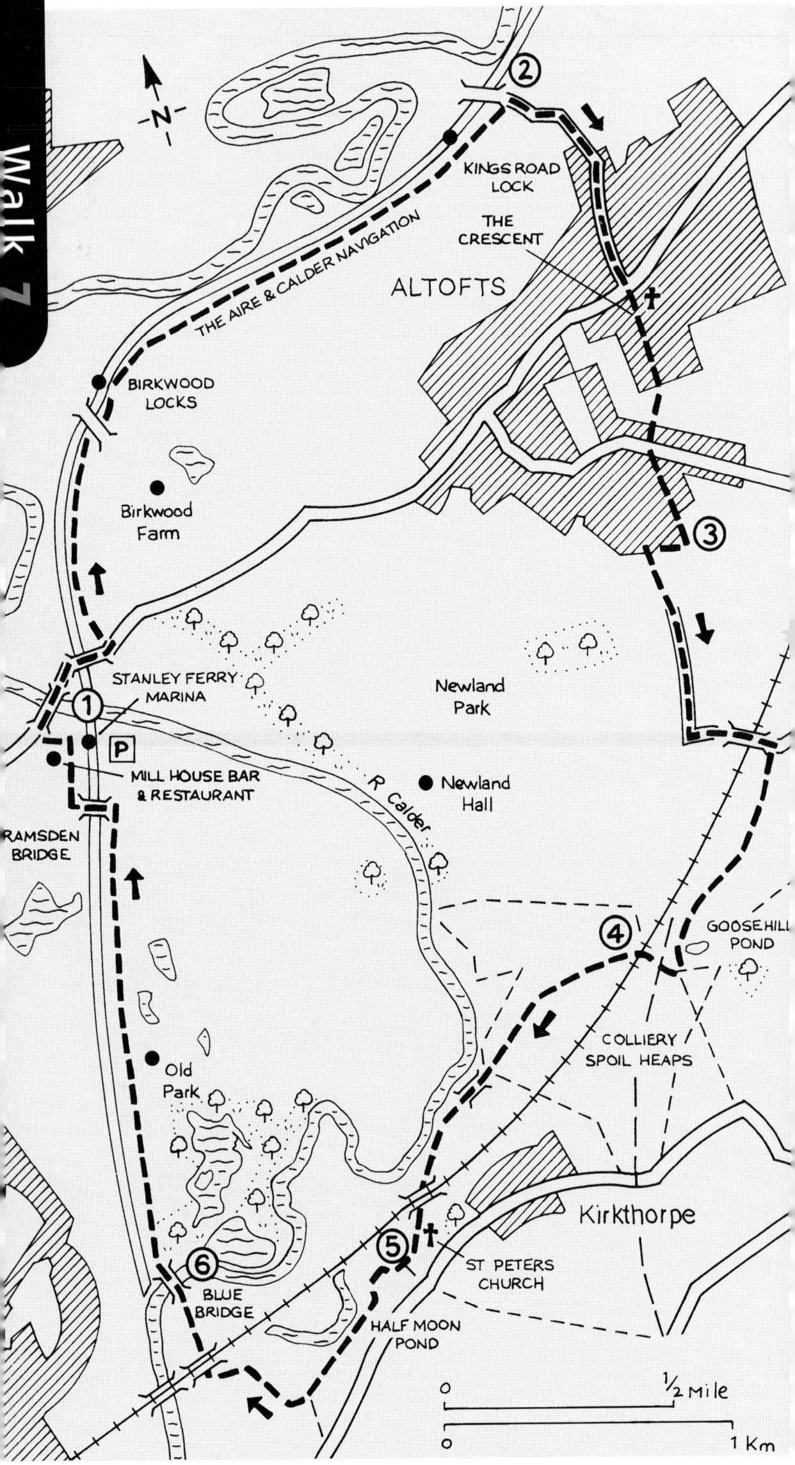

N

② KINGS ROAD LOCK

THE CRESCENT

THE AIRE & CALDER NAVIGATION

ALTOFTS

✝

③

BIRKWOOD LOCKS

Birkwood Farm

Newland Park

① STANLEY FERRY MARINA

R Calder

Newland Hall

P

MILL HOUSE BAR & RESTAURANT

RAMSDEN BRIDGE

④

GOOSEHILL POND

COLLIERY SPOIL HEAPS

Old Park

Kirkthorpe

⑥ BLUE BRIDGE

⑤

✝ ST PETERS CHURCH

HALF MOON POND

0 ½ Mile

0 1 Km

Walk 7 Directions

① Park at the **Stanley Ferry Marina**. Turn right, along the road which crosses first the **River Calder**, then the canal: the **Aire and Calder Navigation**. Take steps to the right, immediately after the canal, to follow the tow path to the right, back under the road bridge. Walk beneath another bridge at **Birkwood Locks**; from here the tow path is metalled. Beyond **Kings Road Lock** you come to a bridge across the canal.

② Don't cross the bridge; turn right instead, on an access road that leads into **Altofts**. Cross the main road and take **The Crescent**, to the right of the church. After 50yds (46m), at the junction with **Priory Close**, take a ginnel ahead between houses. Keep right when you come to a playing field, on a metalled path to a road. Cross here, and take the road ahead (to the left of a chemist's shop). After 50yds (46m), go left down another ginnel. Keep straight ahead to open fields.

③ Go right, along a field-edge path to the end of a cul-de-sac. Go left here, on a path between fields. Cross a tiny stream and continue up the edge of the next field, with a hedgerow to your right. Soon you have a chain-link fence to your left, as you join a metalled track that soon bears left across a railway line. Bear immediately right after the bridge on to a good track. Pass beneath the legs of an electricity pylon, cross a mine access road and keep to the right around **Goosehill Pond**. Bear right, uphill to a lane; go right again, through old gateposts and cross both arms of the railway line.

④ Go through a kissing gate and join a gravel track ahead, across landscaped spoil heaps. When the track forks, by a gate, keep left – to walk parallel to the railway line. As you come to the top of a rise, keep left as the track forks again, to descend with pools either side, to cross a stream on a plank bridge. Bear left at a T-junction of tracks, soon following a narrow path parallel to the river. Keep right beyond a gap in a chain-link fence through woodland. Go beneath the railway line, keeping right up a lane to **St Peter's Church**, Kirkthorpe, in its tranquil setting.

⑤ Keep right, after the church, and right again when you meet a road. Go left after 50yds (46m) on to a track that soon narrows to a woodland path. Beyond **Half Moon Pond** the path forks. Go right (signed 'Stanley Ferry'), through a gate, to the bottom of the hill, where there is another choice of paths. Go right here, gaining the top of an embankment, and soon descending to go beneath the railway again. A good track leads you to the **Blue Bridge**, over the **River Calder**, at the lock where the **Aire and Calder Navigation** begins.

⑥ After the bridge your route is to follow the canal (unless you want to investigate the **Southern Washland Nature Reserve** – signposted to the right - before returning to the canalside path). Cross the canal at Ramsden Bridge, pass the **Mill House** and return to the car park.

Bardsey and Pompocali

A rolling landscape with Roman echoes.

•DISTANCE•	3½ miles (5.7km)
•MINIMUM TIME•	2hrs
•ASCENT / GRADIENT•	164ft (50m) ▲▲▲
•LEVEL OF DIFFICULTY•	🚶🚶 🚶 🚶
•PATHS•	Good paths and tracks (though some, being bridleways, may be muddy), 8 stiles
•LANDSCAPE•	Arable and woodland
•SUGGESTED MAP•	aqua3 OS Explorer 289 Leeds
•START / FINISH•	Grid reference: SE 369430
•DOG FRIENDLINESS•	Keep on lead around Bardsey and while crossing A58
•PARKING•	Lay-by on A58, immediately south of Bardsey
•PUBLIC TOILETS•	None on route

The Romans built a network of important roads across Yorkshire. They provided good transport links between their most important forts, such as Ilkley (probably their Olicana), Tadcaster (Calcaria) and York (Eboracum). And one of these roads, marked on old maps as Ryknield Street, passed close to the village of Bardsey continuing west to a small Roman camp established at Adel. You walk a short stretch of the old Roman road when you take the track from Hetchell Wood, a local nature reserve.

Stirring Remains

Adjacent to these woods – and marked on the Ordnance Survey map as Pompocali – are a set of intriguing earthworks. Though rather overgrown, they still have the power to stir the imagination, not least because they are unencumbered by signs and information panels. A number of Roman finds have been unearthed here, including a quern for grinding corn and a stone altar dedicated to the god Apollo. And a couple of miles away, at Dalton Parlours, the site of a large Roman villa has been discovered.

Once the Romans had abandoned this northern outpost of their empire, Bardsey became part of the kingdom of Elmet, and was later mentioned in the Domesday Book. By the 13th century, the village had been given to the monks of Kirkstall Abbey. After the dissolution of the monasteries, in 1539, Bardsey came under the control of powerful local families – notably the Lords Bingley. The Parish Church of All Hallows, visited towards the end of this walk, is another antiquity – the core of the building is Anglo Saxon.

Above the church is a grassy mound, where a castle once stood. From pottery found on the site, it was occupied during the 12th and 13th centuries, after which it was abandoned. Some of the stonework from the castle was incorporated into the fabric of Bardsey Grange, whose most notable inhabitant was William Congreve. Born here in 1670, Congreve went on to write a number of Restoration comedies for the stage, such as *The Way of the World*.

So close to the city, yet retaining its own identity, Bardsey has expanded beyond its ancient centre to become a popular commuter village for people who work in Leeds. It joins that elite group of places that lay claim to having the country's oldest pub. The Bingley Arms has better claims than most; there is documentary evidence of brewers and innkeepers going back a thousand years. Bardsey is, in short, a historic little spot.

Walk 8 Directions

① From the lay-by, walk past metal bollards into the woods. Join the old railway trackbed, going right, for just a few paces, before bearing left, over a stile, to continue on a woodland path. Soon you are on a field-edge path, with a fence to your left and a thorny hedgerow to your right. Keep straight ahead when the fence ends. When the hedge turns to the right, follow it, and **Bardsey Beck**, downhill.

② Across a stile, you enter **Hetchell Wood**. Keep right, on a good path through the woods, soon passing beneath **Hetchell Crags**, whose soft gritstone façade offers a challenge to local climbers. You soon come to a meeting of paths, close to some stepping stones over the beck.

Don't cross the beck, but go left for a few paces, through a kissing gate, and join a track (of Roman origin) going uphill. (Point Ⓐ on Walk 9).

③ Go right, almost immediately, over a stile. The path goes right, around the earthworks (marked on the map as **Pompocali**), but first you should take five minutes to investigate these intriguing remains. Pass between a stream and an over-hanging rock; take a stile next to a gate. Walk uphill to pass ruinous mill buildings, take another stile, and join a good track that takes you under the old railway line. Immediately after crossing a stream, go through a small gate and walk across a small field to another gate. Beyond the main gate to **Moat Hall**, follow a track for just 20yds (18m), and take a step stile in the wall on your right (Point Ⓑ on Walk 9).

WHILE YOU'RE THERE
At nearby **Bramham Park** you will find a splendid Queen Anne mansion built in 1698. The gardens were laid out by Robert Benson, 1st Lord Bingley, with grand vistas in the manner of Versailles. Visits to the house are by appointment only, but the gardens are open from February to September. The park plays host each year to a three-day cross-country horse racing event.

At the top of the hill, walk downhill for 75yds (68m). Where the hedge ends you meet a cross-track. Ignore the good track ahead and go left here on a track that follows a wall to meet the A58 road.

⑤ Walk left for just 20yds (18m) and bear right on to **Wayside Mount**, an unsurfaced access road that serves a collection of detached houses. Beyond the last house go through a gate and follow the track ahead, with a tall hedge on your left. When the track bears left walk ahead down a field-edge path, following a hedge on the left. Bear half right, near the bottom of the field, to join a narrow path through scrubland, over a little beck, and up to a gate into the churchyard. Keep right of the church to meet a road.

⑥ Go right on **Church Lane** to the A58. Go right for 100yds (91m) to find the lay-by and your car.

WHERE TO EAT AND DRINK
The **Bingley Arms**, on Church Lane, Bardsey, is a contender for the title of the oldest pub in England. The pub – parts of it, at least – is supposed to date back to the year 950, when it was known as the Priests Inn. The pub certainly has charm, excellent food and, in summer, barbecues on the terrace.

④ Take a field-edge path, with a hedge to the right (from here back to **Bardsey** you are walking the **Leeds Country Way**). Towards the far end of the field your path bears right into a copse. Cross a stile and a beck on a little wooden footbridge. Go left, as you leave the copse, and immediately left again on to a hollow way hemmed in by hedgerows. Follow this path through scrubland, past a couple of small fishing lakes, to emerge at a field. Continue up a field-edge path, keeping a hedge to your right.

WHAT TO LOOK FOR
Bardsey's church is like a time capsule of architectural styles. The original Anglo-Saxon building was small: just the nave we see today. Over the next thousand years the building went through many changes. The old Saxon porch was extended into a bell tower, aisles were added in Norman times and in the 19th century the nave walls were heightened to support a new roof.

Bardsey and Thorner

Extend the walk to Thorner, along a stretch of the Leeds Country Way.
See map and information panel for Walk 8

•DISTANCE•	7 miles (11.3km)
•MINIMUM TIME•	3hrs 30min
•ASCENT / GRADIENT•	164ft (50m)
•LEVEL OF DIFFICULTY•	

Walk 9 Directions (Walk 8 option)

From Point Ⓐ keep walking up the sunken track, with a fence left and Roman earthworks right. Go through a gate and cross a minor road; rejoin the path and squeeze past a gate. Your path is now along a field-edge. Bear right to enter **Stubbing Moor Plantation**. The track hugs the left-hand edge. Bear right at the end of the wood and after 20yds (18m) keep left at a fork. Follow this path to a three-way finger post. Bear right through **Ragdale Plantation**, soon following **Milner Beck**. At the next waymarker ignore a path ahead. Go right, following the field-edge uphill. Towards the top of the rise bear left on to **Kennels Lane**. Ignore a side-turn to pass a barn and after ½ mile (800m) of level walking turn left through a gap in the hedge by a fingerpost, signed 'footpath to Thorner'. Follow the hedge on your right, into the valley. At the end of the field, take steps down into woodland and cross a bridge over **Milner Beck**. Bear right, following the beck, soon leaving the wood by a stile. Keep on the path ahead, uphill across pasture. Follow a hedge then head for a stile.

Cross it and follow a hedgerow on your right; cut off the corner of the field and take a kissing gate to a road by a house. Go left to a T-junction in **Thorner**. Go right here, passing the parish church.

About 150yds (138m) past the church, and immediately before the Mexborough Arms, turn right into **Carr Lane**. When the road bears to the left continue ahead – in front of **Victory Hall** – on a track (from here back to **Bardsey** you are following the **Leeds Country Way**). Take two kissing gates in quick succession and join a sunken track following a hedgerow on your right. At the end of the hedge continue downhill at the field edge into the bottom of a valley. Cross a beck, go through a kissing gate, and walk up the middle of the field. Keep to the right of **Oaklands Manor** to take a stile and join a walled path past the house. Come out to a road by some houses. Bear right here, then left in front of a handsome farmhouse.

Follow this road downhill. After crossing a stream, go uphill. At the top of the rise, where the road goes left, bear right, by a white-painted house, on to a gravel track. 50yds (46m) before the gate to **Moat Hall**, take a stile on your left and rejoin Walk 8 at Point Ⓑ.

Walk 10

The Lakes of Walton Heronry

A short walk around a country park and the home of a visionary naturalist.

•DISTANCE•	3½ miles (5.7km)
•MINIMUM TIME•	2hrs
•ASCENT / GRADIENT•	98ft (30m)
•LEVEL OF DIFFICULTY•	
•PATHS•	Good paths and tracks throughout, canal tow path, 4 stiles
•LANDSCAPE•	Country park, lakes, woodland and canal
•SUGGESTED MAP•	aqua3 OS explorer 278 Sheffield & Barnsley
•START / FINISH•	Grid reference: SE 375153
•DOG FRIENDLINESS•	Good, but care should be taken when near wildfowl
•PARKING•	Walton Heronry and Anglers Country Park on Haw Park Lane, between Crofton and Ryehill
•PUBLIC TOILETS•	At visitor centre, at start of walk

Walk 10 Directions

Few houses are situated as delightfully as Walton Hall, built in 1767 on its own little island, surrounded by a lake, with just a cast iron bridge to link it to the 'mainland'. Walton Hall was the home of a man who deserves to be better known. Charles Waterton was a man ahead of his time. He was viewed, during his lifetime, as an eccentric figure, though his interest in environmental issues would put him in the vanguard of 'green' thinking if he were alive today.

Born in 1782, Charles Waterton was a keen naturalist, whose interest flourished with visits to Guyana and Brazil. He returned to Walton Hall with many exotic specimens (now displayed in Wakefield Museum) and created, on his estate, what was probably the world's first nature reserve. He prohibited shooting and built hides.

For the next 40 years he planted trees, conserved the wildlife and made nesting boxes for birds (another world's first, apparently). He built a high wall around the estate, to keep the poachers out and the wildlife in. He funded this unusual project, he said from 'the wine I do not drink'. When he died, in 1865, he was buried in the woods he loved. Ironically, his son, Edmund, subsequently hosted shooting parties in the estate, to help to pay off his debts. You can cross the iron bridge to the Georgian hall, though it has been converted to become the Waterton Park Hotel. You can enjoy a drink or meal on the lawn, with the lake as a backdrop.

WHAT TO LOOK FOR ⓘ

In a **heronry**, it makes sense to look out for herons. The tall, grey heron is one of Britain's most easily recognised birds. At one time it was believed the heron's skill at catching fish must be due to magical substances in its legs.

> ### *WHERE TO EAT AND DRINK* ⓘ
> Not many pubs sit on an island like **Waterton Park Hotel**. It's not your average hiker's pub, but where else will you have the opportunity to eat and drink in such beautiful surroundings? A more modest café can be found in the **visitor centre** by the car park.

The Heronry is the name which Wakefield Countryside Service has given to a fascinating collection of lakes, woods and open parkland, including Anglers Country Park, Wintersett Reservoir and Walton Hall. As is often the case in the south east of the county, some of these lakes were originally dug for opencast mining. Part of the walk accompanies the Barnsley Canal, opened in 1799 and mainly used for the transport of coal. Once the railway had come, the canal was abandoned. Charles Waterton would approve of the way it is 'going back to nature'. The visitor centre, next to the car park, has toilets, a café and an interactive exhibition about Squire Waterton's life and work.

From the car park, take the track past the visitor centre towards the main lake. Bear left, at a fork of tracks, to walk near the water's edge. Having left the lake behind, look out for a stile in the fence to your left. Notice the waymarked sign – '**Waterton Trail**' – here and at many other points on the walk.

Join a field path, keeping a fence to your right. Cross two fields in the same direction towards a golf course. After you take a pair of stiles and a tiny footbridge in quick succession, bear half right across the next field. As you leave this field via a stile, bear sharp left to follow a grassy track along the fringe of the

golf course. Pass a small pond, and enter woodland. The obvious path stays close to the edge of the wood and soon follows a lake on your left. Leave woodland on a stony track with views over the lake and **Walton Hall Hotel** on its island. As you approach another golf hole you will have to make some minor detours (follow the signs) as you approach the hotel complex.

Keep right along a track, towards woodland, but then go immediately left on a grassy track. When you meet a more substantial track, follow it left, for 75yds (68m). Bear left after a fence on a grassy path uphill through scrubland. Go through a gap in a brick wall, turning left to follow the wall. Meet the hotel's access road and go right. At the top of the hill, just before the golfers' clubhouse, bear left to join the tow path of the **Barnsley Canal**.

When the path forks, go right, uphill, to cross a bridge over the canal. Bear right to follow a good track, still following the canal. When the track forks again, keep left. Follow the boundary wall of the **Walton Estate** into woodland. Keep left by an information panel and leave the woodland through a gate. Walk uphill on a stony track which soon becomes a metalled access road. Follow it back to the **Heronry** car park.

> ### *WHILE YOU'RE THERE* ⓘ
> Nearby **Nostell Priory** is a magnificent house built in 1733 on the site of a medieval priory. It is home to art treasures, paintings and tapestries – with a particularly fine collection of Chippendale furniture. There are extensive grounds and gardens, with a scented rose garden and peaceful lakeside walks.

Harewood's Treasure House

A stately home with parkland by 'Capability' Brown, a few miles from Leeds.

•DISTANCE•	6½ miles (10.4km)
•MINIMUM TIME•	3hrs
•ASCENT / GRADIENT•	164ft (50m) ▲ ▲ ▲
•LEVEL OF DIFFICULTY•	🚶 🚶 🚶
•PATHS•	Good paths and parkland tracks all the way, 2 stiles
•LANDSCAPE•	Arable and parkland
•SUGGESTED MAP•	aqua3 OS Explorer 289 Leeds
•START / FINISH•	Grid reference: SE 332450
•DOG FRIENDLINESS•	Keep under control through estate and on A658
•PARKING•	Limited in Harewood village. From traffic lights, take A658, and park in first lay-by on left
•PUBLIC TOILETS•	None on route; in Harewood House if you pay to go in

BACKGROUND TO THE WALK

The grand old houses of West Yorkshire tend to be in the form of 'Halifax' houses (such as East Riddlesden Hall, ► Walk 45). Self-made yeomen and merchant clothiers built their mansions, to show the world that they'd made their 'brass'. But Harewood House, on the edge of Leeds, is more ambitious, and is still one of the great treasure houses of England.

Vision into Reality

The Harewood Estate passed through a number of wealthy hands during the 16th and 17th centuries, eventually being bought by the Lascelles family who still own the house today. Edwin Lascelles left the 12th-century castle in its ruinous state, to overlook the broad valley of the River Wharfe, but demolished the old hall. He wanted to create something very special in its place and hired the best architects and designers to turn his vision into reality.

John Carr of York created a veritable palace of a house, in an imposing neo-classical style and laid out the estate village of Harewood too. The interior of the building was designed by Robert Adam, now best remembered for his fireplaces. Thomas Chippendale, born in nearby Otley, made furniture for every room, as part of the house's original plans. The foundations were laid in 1759; 12 years later the house was finished. Inside the house are paintings by JMW Turner and Thomas Girtin, who both stayed and painted at the house. Turner was particularly taken with the area, producing pictures of many local landmarks. The sumptuous interior, full of family portraits, ornate plasterwork and silk hangings, is in sharp contrast to life below stairs, in the kitchen and scullery.

The house sits in extensive grounds, which were preened and groomed to be every bit as magnificent as the house. They were shaped by Lancelot 'Capability' Brown, the most renowned designer of the English landscape. In addition to the formal gardens, he created the lake and the woodland paths you will take on this walk. Like so many of England's stateliest homes, Harewood House has had to earn its keep in recent years. The bird garden was the first commercial venture, but now the house hosts events such as art exhibitions, vintage car rallys and even open-air concerts. This would make a good morning walk, with lunch at the Harewood Arms – perhaps followed by a tour of the house itself.

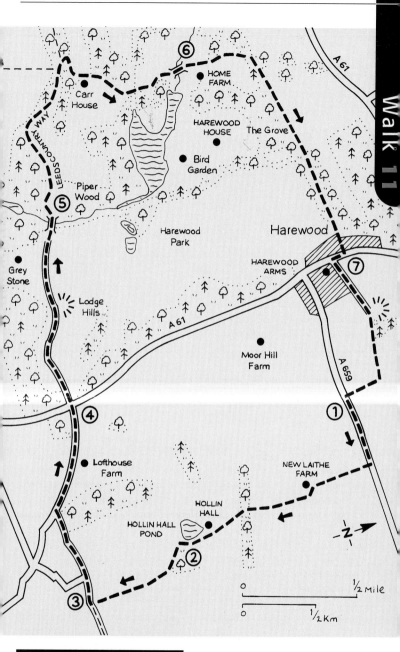

Walk 11 Directions

① From the lay-by walk 50yds (46m) away from the village of **Harewood**, cross the road and walk right, down the access track to

New Laithe Farm. Keep to the left of the farm buildings, on a grassy track heading into the valley bottom. Go through two gates and bear half left up a field, towards **Hollin Hall**. Keep left of the buildings to pass **Hollin Hall Pond**.

Walk 11

② Beyond the pond take a gate and follow a track to the left, uphill, skirting woodland. Continue uphill on a field-edge path with a hedgerow to your left. Pass through two gates, the path now being enclosed between hedges.

③ Bear right at the top of the hill to have easy, level walking on an enclosed sandy track (you are now joining the **Leeds Country Way**). Keep straight ahead when the track forks, through a gate. Skirt woodland to emerge at a road; bear right here to arrive at the main A61.

> **WHILE YOU'RE THERE**
> While the walk described here uses rights of way through the grounds of **Harewood House**, you need to pay if you want to investigate the house itself, or the bird gardens, or the many other attractions. Make a day of it: do the walk in the morning, have lunch at the Harewood Arms and investigate the unrivalled splendour of Harewood House in the afternoon.

④ Cross the road to enter the **Harewood Estate** (via the right-hand gate, between imposing gate-posts). Follow the broad track ahead, through landscaped parkland, soon getting views of **Harewood House** to the right. Enter woodland through a gate, bearing immediately left after a stone bridge.

⑤ Bear right after 100yds (91m), as the track forks. At a crossing of tracks, bear right, downhill, still through woodland. At the next two forks keep first right, then left, to pass a farm. Follow a good track down towards the lake. Go through a gate, keep left of a high brick wall and walk uphill to join a metalled access road to the left.

> **WHERE TO EAT AND DRINK**
> Apart from designing the house itself, John Carr was also responsible for the estate village of Harewood. The neat terraced houses, though modest by comparison, have architectural echoes of the big house. Almost opposite the main gates of Harewood House is the **Harewood Arms**, a former coaching inn that offers the chance of a drink or meal towards the end of the walk. If the weather is kind, you can rest your legs in the beer garden.

Walk down past a house and keep straight ahead at crossroads. Cross a bridge and follow the lane up to a gate, soon passing **Home Farm** (now converted to business units).

⑥ Follow the road through pastureland, keeping right, uphill, at a choice of routes. Continue through woodland until you come to the few houses that comprise the estate village of **Harewood**.

⑦ Cross the main A61 road and walk right, for just 50yds (46m), to take a metalled drive immediately before the **Harewood Arms**. Pass **Maltkiln House**, keeping straight on, through a gate, as the road becomes a track. Enjoy great views over **Lower Wharfedale**. After a stile by a gate, take another stile in the fence to your right and follow a field path back to the A659 road and your car.

> **WHAT TO LOOK FOR**
> The **red kite**, a beautiful fork-tailed bird of prey, used to be a familiar sight. But the numbers had dwindled to just a few pairs, mostly in Wales, due to centuries of persecution. There is now a new initiative to reintroduce the red kite to Yorkshire, and a number of birds have been released at Harewood House. You may be lucky enough to spot one.

Discovering the Rural Side of Leeds

From the bustle of the city to the heart of the country.

•DISTANCE•	5 miles (8km)
•MINIMUM TIME•	2hrs 30min
•ASCENT / GRADIENT•	98ft (30m)
•LEVEL OF DIFFICULTY•	
•PATHS•	Urban ginnels, parkland and woodland paths, 2 stiles
•LANDSCAPE•	Mostly woodland
•SUGGESTED MAP•	aqua3 OS Explorers 289 Leeds, 297 Lower Wharfedale
•START•	Grid reference: SE 294352 (on Explorer 289)
•FINISH•	Grid reference: SE 270402 (on Explorer 297)
•DOG FRIENDLINESS•	Good, but watch for traffic early on
•PARKING•	Free parking on Raglan Road, just off the A660, at eastern end of Woodhouse Moor
•PUBLIC TOILETS•	Meanwood Park

BACKGROUND TO THE WALK

This, the only linear walk in the book, is a splendid ramble, surprisingly rural in aspect throughout, even though it begins just a stone's throw from the bustling heart of Leeds. You start among the terraces of red-brick houses that are so typical of the city, and five minutes later you are in delightful woodland.

Linking with the Dales Way
The walk follows the first 5 miles (8km) of the Dales Way link path from Leeds to Ilkley (the walk's official starting point). This link path begins at Woodhouse Moor – where fairs and circuses have long pitched their tents – so we shall do the same. The path follows first Woodhouse Ridge, then the Hollies and the Meanwood Valley, the path cocooned against creeping suburbia by a slim sliver of woodland. The route is also being promoted as the Meanwood Valley Trail, so there are waymarkers to guide you at every point of indecision.

Parklife
Leeds is fortunate to have so many parks within the city limits: long-established green spaces such as Roundhay Park, and newer parks created from 'brownfield' sites. The first few miles of this walk are through some of this pleasant parkland. Then, having crossed beneath the Leeds Ring Road, you have the more natural surroundings of Adel Woods to enjoy.

The walk finishes near Adel church, dedicated to St John the Baptist. Though small, it is one of the most perfectly proportioned Norman churches in the country, having been built about 1170. The ornamental stone carving is noteworthy – especially the four arches framing the doorway. From here there's a reliable bus service back to Woodhouse Moor. To lengthen the walk by 1½ miles (2.4km), don't turn left down Stairfoot Lane (at Point ⑤), but take the track ahead, and turn left when you come to King Lane. This will bring you out at Golden Acre Park, near Bramhope (on the same bus route for getting back to Leeds).

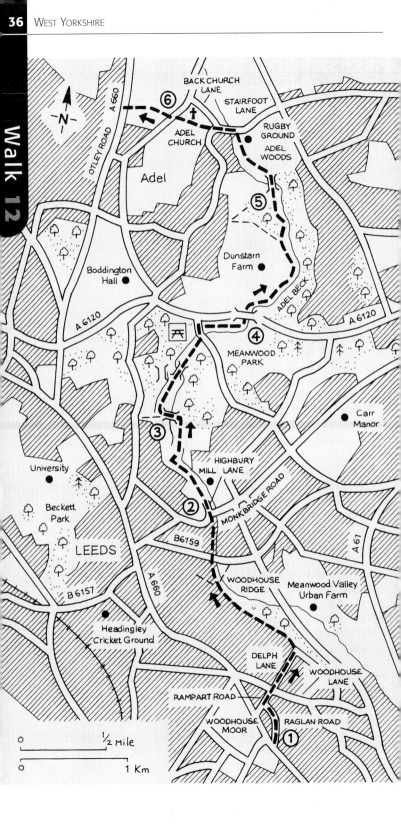

Walk 12 right margin

Walk 12 Directions

① Walk down **Raglan Road** and turn right on to **Rampart Road**. Cross **Woodhouse Lane**, and walk ahead up **Delph Lane**. When the road ends at a wall, take a gate and walk left along **Woodhouse Ridge**. Don't be side-tracked; keep to the obvious path, with woodland to your right and a high wall to your left. At a barrier take the middle option, then up and down some steps, and across a road, continuing in the same direction. This ginnel emerges at **Monkbridge Road**.

② Cross the road, and take **Highbury Lane** ahead – soon recovering the path, which now accompanies **Meanwood Beck**. As you pass a mill follow a path first left, then right, beyond the mill dam. Walk between allotments and past a cricket ground, to join a road for just 100yds (91m). Bear right, in front of a post box, through stone gate-posts, to enter **Meanwood Park**. Bear left, beyond a small car park, on a metalled lane through the park, to a short row of terraced houses known as **Hustlers Row**.

③ Keep left of the houses as the lane becomes a stony track. Cross **Meanwood Beck** on a footbridge, bearing right at a fork of tracks to follow the beck into woodland. Cross a side-beck, to have this watercourse on your left and the beck on your right. Ignore side-tracks and a footbridge on the left to arrive at a double bridge. Cross the beck to your right, and continue to follow its course. Go right at a stile 50yds (46m) beyond the bridge, and immediately left to follow a field-edge path. Meet a road by a picnic site and

information panel. Go left along the road. Just 20yds (18m) from the ring road, go right on a metalled track which soon continues as a path. Beyond a paddock go left through a tunnel beneath the road.

④ Take steps, at the far end, on to a path that follows **Adel Beck**. Keep left of the next pile of boulders, on a path through woodland. After a small pond go right, downhill, alongside an aqueduct into **Adel Woods**. Keep right at the next fork and cross a stony track to another meeting of tracks.

⑤ Walk straight ahead, cross the beck on a stone bridge, and take steps uphill to a pond. Keep to the right-hand path, past a rugby ground – soon reaching a car park and a minor road, **Stairfoot Lane**. Go left down the road; this sunken lane soon rises to a junction. Go right on to **Back Church Lane**. When the road bears right, keep straight on to follow the wall on your left and access a track that takes you straight to **Adel church**.

⑥ Walk past the church and leave the churchyard by a collection of coffins and millstones. Cross the road and take a field path opposite. Bear half left across the next field to the **Otley Road** (A660). Turn left to find a bus stop, opposite a petrol station, for the bus back to **Woodhouse Moor**, in Leeds.

WHERE TO EAT AND DRINK ℹ

There are several pubs just off-route during this walk. But the simplest option is to wait until the finishing point, where you will find the **Lawnswood Arms**. Your car is parked close to the university, so you will find cheap and cheerful curry houses nearby, and some characterful city pubs.

Golden Acre and Breary Marsh

A walk of great variety in the rolling countryside to the north of Leeds.

·DISTANCE·	5 miles (8km)
·MINIMUM TIME·	2hrs 30min
·ASCENT / GRADIENT·	100ft (30m) ▲
·LEVEL OF DIFFICULTY·	🚶🚶
·PATHS·	Good paths, tracks and quiet roads, 21 stiles
·LANDSCAPE·	Parkland, woods and arable country
·SUGGESTED MAP·	aqua3 OS Explorer 297 Lower Wharfedale
·START / FINISH·	Grid reference: SE 266418
·DOG FRIENDLINESS·	On lead when in park, due to wildfowl
·PARKING·	Golden Acre Park car park, across road from park itself, on A660 just south of Bramhope
·PUBLIC TOILETS·	Golden Acre Park, at start of walk

BACKGROUND TO THE WALK

Leeds is fortunate to have so many green spaces. Some, like Roundhay Park, are long established; others, like the Kirkstall Valley nature reserve, have been created from post-industrial wasteland. But none have had a more chequered history than Golden Acre Park, 6 miles (9.7km) north of the city on the main A660.

Amusement Park

The park originally opened in 1932 as an amusement park. The attractions included a miniature railway, nearly 2 miles (3.2km) in length, complete with dining car. The lake was the centre of much activity, with motor launches, dinghies for hire and races by the Yorkshire Hydroplane Racing Squadron. An open-air lido known, somewhat exotically, as the Blue Lagoon, offered unheated swimming and the prospect of goose-pimples. The Winter Gardens Dance Hall boasted that it had 'the largest dance floor in Yorkshire'.

Though visitors initially flocked to Golden Acre Park, the novelty soon wore off. By the end of the 1938 season the amusement park had closed down and was sold to Leeds City Council. The site was subsequently transformed into botanical gardens – a process that's continued ever since. The hillside overlooking the lake has been lovingly planted with trees and unusual plants, including rock gardens and fine displays of rhododendrons.

The boats are long gone; the lake is now a haven for wildfowl. Within these 127 acres (51ha) – the 'Golden Acre' name was as fanciful as 'the Blue Lagoon' – is a wide variety of wildlife habitats, from open heathland to an old quarry. Lovers of birds, trees and flowers will find plenty to interest them at every season of the year. One of the few echoes of the original Golden Acre Park is a café situated close to the entrance.

Reflecting the park's increasing popularity with local people, a large car park has been built on the opposite side of the main road, with pedestrian access to the park via a tunnel beneath the road. This intriguing park offers excellent walking, and wheelchair users, too, can make a circuit of the lake on a broad path.

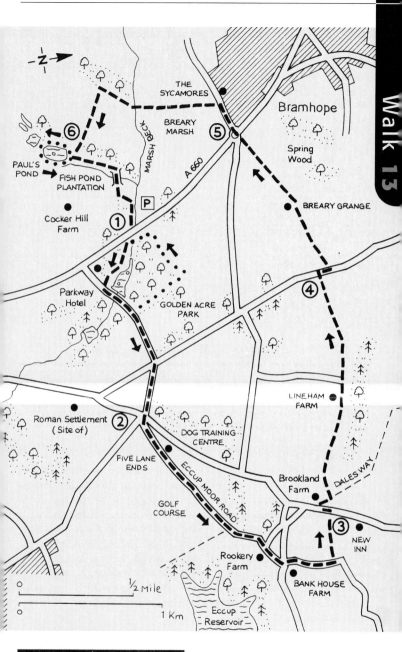

Walk 13 Directions

① From the far left end of the car park, take steps and an underpass beneath the road, into **Golden Acre Park**. Take one of the paths to the

left or the right around the lake; at the far left end of the lake leave the park by a gate (signed '**Meanwood Valley Trail**'). Bear left, along a tree-lined path, to a T-junction of roads. Take the road ahead, up to the aptly-named **Five Lane Ends**.

Walk 13

② Take the second road on the left (**Eccup Moor Road**), passing a dog training centre on the left and a golf course on the right. Ignore side turnings till you reach the outbuildings of **Bank House Farm**, where you take a farm track to the left. It soon narrows to become a path between hedgerows. About 50yds (46m) before the footpath bears right take a stile in the fence on your left, to join a field path to a wall stile. Cross another field to meet a road (the **New Inn** is just along the road to your right).

WHAT TO LOOK FOR
Look for the damp-loving alder trees in Breary Marsh. Their seeds are designed to float on the water. During winter you should see little siskins (a type of finch) feeding on the seeds, of which they are particularly fond. You may also spy the vivid caterpillar of the alder moth.

③ Go left along the road for just 20yds (18m) to take a stile on your right (signposted 'Dales Way'), leading to a field path. After another stile you join a track ahead over a further stile and uphill with a wall to your left. Veer right across pasture to a wall stile and continue towards **Lineham Farm**. Beyond two more wall stiles you pass the farm buildings and join a good track. When the track goes left you keep straight ahead on a path between fences. After field-edge walking, and a further three stiles, you reach a road.

④ Go right along the road for 150yds (138m) and take a waymarked stile on the left by a gate. Follow the field-edge path with a fence on your left. Through two kissing gates bear left across a field, keeping to the right of **Breary Grange Farm**. After a ladder stile,

WHERE TO EAT AND DRINK
It requires the shortest of detours, at about the half-way point of this walk, to visit the **New Inn**, near Eccup. A sign welcomes walkers – as do the open fires and beer garden – and an extensive menu will whet your appetite.

cross a field to the bottom right-hand corner and another stile. Head left, across the next field, to a stile, that brings you out at the A660 by a roundabout.

⑤ Cross the main road and take **The Sycamores** ahead. After 250yds (230m) take a waymarked stile on the left to join a field-edge footpath with a hedge on the left. Cross a succession of five stiles, and then tiny Marsh Beck, before skirting an area of woodland on your right. Beyond a ladder stile you join a farm track, bearing left past a farmhouse to enter **Fish Pond Plantation** via a gate.

⑥ Bear right, through the wood, soon reaching the retaining wall of a small stretch of water known locally as **Paul's Pond**. Bear left here on a woodland path accompanying a stream. Having crossed the stream on a footbridge, you soon join a duck-boarded walkway that keeps you dry-footed as you cross **Breary Marsh**. The walkway meanders back towards the underpass beneath the A660 road. Go left, in front of it, back into the car park.

WHILE YOU'RE THERE
Take a look at Bramhope's **Puritan Chapel**, adjacent to the entrance to the Post House Hotel on the A660, as it passes through the village. This small, simple chapel was built in 1649, by devout Puritan Robert Dyneley. It contains original furnishings, including box-pews and a three-deck pulpit.

A Haven for Birds

A short wildlife walk around Golden Acre Park and Breary Marsh.
See map and information panel for Walk 13

•DISTANCE•	2½ miles (4km)
•MINIMUM TIME•	1hr 30min
•ASCENT / GRADIENT•	100ft (30m) ▲ ▲ ▲
•LEVEL OF DIFFICULTY•	🚶 🚶 🚶

Walk 14 Directions (Walk 13 option)

Golden Acre Park is justifiably popular with people who live to the north of Leeds. A short walk around the park can be taken, following the waymarked trails, or just wandering freely. You can make a pleasant circuit by following Walk 13 to the far side of the lake then doubling back on **The Valley** and **Plantation Walks**.

The park offers a variety of habitats for attracting birds. The lake is the most obvious focus, with a resident flock of waterfowl. An identification board will help you to put names to the ducks, geese, gulls and swans that come to feed on visitors' bread. Other, rarer species may also be seen. Great crested grebes perform elaborate mating rituals during the nesting season. Whooper swans fly down from Scandinavia to winter here. During the spring and autumn migration, many species of water birds make fleeting visits. The sloping woodlands, criss-crossed by paths, are the ideal habitat for woodpeckers, nuthatches and treecreepers. In summer these trees are filled with songbirds, including many melodious species

of warbler. At the highest point of the park is an old quarry; look here for rock pipits and wagtails. An area of heathland, bursting with colour each summer from flowering gorse bushes, is where you will find linnets, yellowhammers and the fluid song of the skylark. In the more formal gardens, near the park's main entrance, you can see garden birds such as blue tits, chaffinches and robins. There is probably nowhere else in West Yorkshire where you could spot so many species of birds in so small an area. This is all the more remarkable when you consider that Golden Acre Park lies within the city boundary of Leeds.

Just across the road from the park (and easily accessible from the car park) is **Breary Marsh**. This is one of West Yorkshire's few remaining wetlands: an area of alder wood, with uncommon damp-loving plants such as tussock sedge and marsh marigold. Access to the site is on raised wooden duckboards; information panels help to identify the flora and fauna. At the far end of **Breary Marsh** is the tranquil little mere known as **Paul's Pond**. Take a stroll around the pond – you may spot a heron or a moorhen – before returning, by the same route, back to the car park.

A Walk around Newmillerdam

A pleasant oasis, close to Wakefield, and a chance to feed the ducks.

•DISTANCE•	4½ miles (7.2km)
•MINIMUM TIME•	2hrs
•ASCENT / GRADIENT•	164ft (50m)
•LEVEL OF DIFFICULTY•	
•PATHS•	Good paths by lake and through woodland, 2 stiles
•LANDSCAPE•	Reservoir, heath and woodland
•SUGGESTED MAP•	aqua3 OS Explorer 278 Sheffield & Barnsley
•START / FINISH•	Grid reference: SE 331157
•DOG FRIENDLINESS•	Can be off lead on most of walk
•PARKING•	Pay-and-display car park at western end of dam, on A61 between Wakefield and Barnsley
•PUBLIC TOILETS•	At start of walk

Walk 15 Directions

Newmillerdam Country Park lies on the A61 near the village of Newmillerdam, and just 3 miles (4.8km) south of Wakefield. The name refers, unsurprisingly, to a 'new mill on the dam' – a mill where people brought their corn to be ground. The lake and woods were created as a park for a 16th-century country house, which has since been demolished. From 1753 the park formed part of the Chevet Estate, which was owned by the Pilkington family. They used the lake for fishing and shooting and,

> **WHERE TO EAT AND DRINK** ⓘ
> **The Dam** – a pub that offers good food, including a carvery – is situated, conveniently and appropriately, by the lake's dam. The **Fox and Hounds**, serving meals all day, and the **Pledwick Well**, which also has a restaurant, make up the trio of pubs in reasonably close proximity to Newmillerdam.

in 1820, built a distinctive boathouse as a place for their guests to socialise and enjoy the lake view. This Grade II listed building has recently been restored and is now used as a visitor centre.

In 1954 Newmillerdam became a public park; local people come here to walk, fish, watch birds or just feed the ducks. The lake is surrounded by woodland. Conifer trees were planted here during the 1950s with the intention, once the trees had reached maturity, to use the wood for making pit props for the coal mines. These trees are mature now but, ironically, the need for the pit props has gone, as most of the Yorkshire pits are closed. The Wakefield Countryside Service is gradually replacing the conifers with broadleaved trees such as oak, ash, birch and hazel, which support a greater variety of birdlife.

A simple circuit of the lake is a pleasant 2-mile (3.2km) stroll, on

WHAT TO LOOK FOR (i)

WHAT TO LOOK FOR
Ducks, geese and swans have no trouble finding food at Newmillerdam, as people with bagfuls of stale bread queue up to feed them. The most common of the ducks you'll see is the mallard, the 'basic' duck. The females are brown and make the satisfying 'quack quack' sounds which delight children. The males have distinctive green heads, yellow bills and grey bodies. Their tone is more nasal and much weaker sounding. Mallards pair off in the late autumn but the males leave egg incubation and rearing of the young to the females.

a track suitable for push-chairs or wheelchairs. But this walk also takes you through **Seckar Wood**, a Site of Special Scientific Interest (SSSI). The woodland comprises a mixture of dry heath, wet heath and scrubland: another habitat rich in wildlife. During the late summer the heathland is a colourful profusion of purple heather.

Walk right, along the A61, to the far side of the lake, to join a path down the eastern side of the lake. Pass the ornate boathouse and a causeway across the lake. Where the lake narrows to a beck, take a bridge across it. Ignore paths to left and right, by walking straight ahead, up into mixed woodland. Bear left when you come to a more substantial track, turning right after 250yds (228m) to take a bridge over the trackbed of an old railway line. Continue on a track ahead, soon

following a chain-link fence on your right, to arrive at the A61 road again. Cross the road and walk right for 250yds (228m) before taking a path left past a metal gate and into **Seckar Wood**. Pass a couple of ponds and make a gradual ascent up through the wood; at the top the trees give way to heather and heathland. Ignore all side-tracks and leave the heath as you meet another path.

Go right here, with a hedge on the left and a wall on the right. Soon you find yourself on a field path. Follow the edge of the wood downhill, as it sweeps right, down to a stile at the bottom of the field. Cross this stile and another immediately after; at the next field keep right until you come to a gap in the hedge. Now follow a grassy path at the field's edge, keeping the hedgerow to your left.

As you approach houses, follow the track and the hedge to the right. At a wide gap in the hedge, go left on a farm track that brings you out on to a road. Go right here, downhill, turning right after 200yds (192m) at a mini-roundabout, on to **Wood Lane**. Just past the **Pennine Camphill Community** take a footpath on the left between a fence and a wall. Meet a minor road by a sharp bend. Walk straight ahead, down the road, to reach the A61. Go left, back down to the car park at **Newmillerdam**.

WHILE YOU'RE THERE (i)

WHILE YOU'RE THERE
Immediately to the north of Newmillerdam is **Pugneys Country Park**, a popular place of recreation with people from Wakefield. A large lake is overlooked by what remains of Sandal Castle, which was, in the words of the old music hall song, 'one of the ruins that Cromwell knocked about a bit'. The original motte and bailey date from the 12th century, the later stone castle from the days of Richard III. He had planned to make Sandal his key permanent stronghold in the north of England before he was killed at the Battle of Bosworth in 1485.

Tong & Fulneck's Moravian Settlement

A little rural oasis between Leeds and Bradford, and some of the finest Georgian architecture in Yorkshire.

•DISTANCE•	4 miles (6.4km)
•MINIMUM TIME•	2hrs
•ASCENT / GRADIENT•	262ft (80m) ▲ ▲ ▲
•LEVEL OF DIFFICULTY•	🚶 🚶 🚶
•PATHS•	Ancient causeways, hollow ways and field paths, 12 stiles
•LANDSCAPE•	Mostly wooded valleys
•SUGGESTED MAP•	aqua3 OS Explorer 288 Bradford & Huddersfield
•START / FINISH•	Grid reference: SE 222306
•DOG FRIENDLINESS•	Can be off lead for most of walk
•PARKING•	Lay-by in Tong village, near church, or on edge of village
•PUBLIC TOILETS•	None on route

BACKGROUND TO THE WALK

West Yorkshire has some rugged moorland walks, where you can lengthen your stride and escape the crowds. Other walks – such as this one – are to be treasured for being so close to town.

Fulneck Moravian Settlement
The Pennine areas of Yorkshire have long been strongholds for non-conformist faiths. The harsh conditions and uncertain livelihoods produced people who were both independent of mind and receptive to radical ideas. Some travelling preachers could fill churches, with congregations overflowing into the churchyard. The Revd William Grimshaw of Haworth, for example, was one such tireless orator. He was always prepared to ride many moorland miles to preach the gospel and – if necessary – to chase drinkers out of the pubs and into church with a horse-whip. Religion was a passionate business in the 18th century and John Wesley found converts here, and imposingly austere Methodist chapels sprang up in the smallest village.

Just to the south of Pudsey is Fulneck, where another non-conformist church found a home. Pre-Reformation dissenters from the Roman Catholic Church, the Moravians, originated in Bohemia in the 15th century, and soon spread to Moravia. During the 18th century, Moravian missionaries were sent overseas to spread the word and one such group arrived in England. They were actually on their way to America, but a meeting with Benjamin Ingham, a Church of England clergyman, encouraged them to settle here.

In 1744 Ingham presented the Moravians with a 22-acre (9-ha) estate for them to use as a centre for their work in Yorkshire. At first they called the settlement Lambshill; then Fulneck, commemorating a town of that name in Moravia. It is a splendid site, high on a ridge with a fine view across Fulneck Valley. The Moravians constructed a street on the ridge, and built a collection of handsome buildings along it. Soon there was a chapel, large communal houses (for single brethren, single sisters and for widows), family houses, a shop, inn, bakery and workshops forming a close-knit, self-sufficient settlement. John Wesley visited Fulneck in 1780 and was suitably impressed by their hard work and independence.

Two schools were built (one for boys, one for girls), originally just for the children of Moravian Brethren. But they were eventually transformed into the fee-paying boarding schools that still exist today. The most famous pupil was probably Richard Oastler who, in the 19th century, campaigned against 'child slavery' in Yorkshire's textile mills.

As close as it is to Pudsey, this terrace of splendid Georgian buildings has retained its air of separateness. The exposed site has discouraged further building, so what you see today is very much as the Moravians originally envisaged. Take the time to explore this evocative place and perhaps visit the museum too, which explains the history of the Moravian Church and this unique Yorkshire outpost.

Tong and Cockers Dale

Apart from visiting the Moravian Community, this short walk also takes you through two delightful valleys: Fulneck Valley and Cockers Dale. In these wooded dells, criss-crossed by ancient packhorse tracks and hollow ways, you can feel a long way from the surrounding cities. On a ridge between these valleys is the village of Tong (the name means 'a spit of land') which has kept its traditional shape and character, and avoided being absorbed by creeping suburbia.

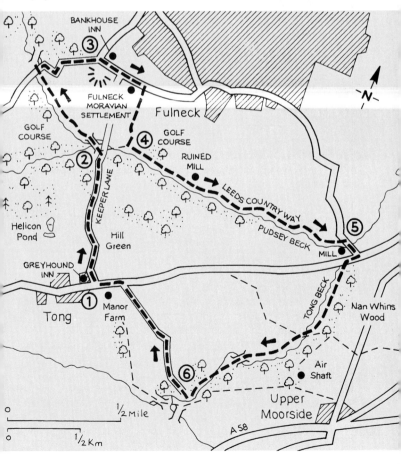

Walk 16

Walk 16 Directions

① From **Tong** village walk up **Keeper Lane** which, beyond a gate, becomes a sandy track. Walk steadily downhill, following a line of old causey stones, into woodland. Cross **Pudsey Beck** on a footbridge.

② After the bridge you have a choice of tracks. As you approach a waymarker post, continue ahead between stone posts, signed as the **Leeds Country Way**. Follow the beck with a golf course on your right. Beyond a stile follow a field path to another stile, a footbridge and a meeting of paths. Don't cross the bridge, but turn sharp right instead, up a farm track. Meet a road by the **Bankhouse Inn**.

WHAT TO LOOK FOR ⓘ

Many of the footpaths in the area follow old packhorse routes: some are secluded sunken lanes, others still have their lines of causey stones (paving slabs) intact. They offer good walking, even in wet weather.

---

③ Follow the road to the right to investigate the fine Georgian buildings that make up the **Fulneck Moravian settlement**, on a ridge with good valley views. 50yds (46m) beyond the **Fulneck Restaurant** go right, down a lane that soon bends to the right. At the bottom of a large brick building look out for

steps and a footpath downhill. Follow this delightful sunken path with hedgerows – and golf fairways – to either side. Come out onto the golf course, keeping half left across a fairway, to rejoin the path accompanying **Pudsey Beck**.

④ After three stiles you reach a ruined mill; bear right here to continue on the beckside path. You have easy walking, through fields and scrubland, punctuated by stiles. Leave the beck via a walled path, which brings you out onto a road.

⑤ Go right here, passing another mill, to a T-junction. Cross the road and take a waymarked footpath between gateposts into **Sykes Wood**. Go right, through a gate (signed '**Leeds Countryside Way**'). Follow the path downhill, soon with **Tong Beck**. After walking about ½ mile (800m) through woodland, take a footbridge over the beck and walk across a field, bearing left to a stile. Follow a path along the edge of a field, then through woodland. Keep left, when the track forks, to a stile. Keep following the track – ignoring bridges and side-paths – till you come to a stile next to a gate and meet a broader track.

⑥ Go right, uphill, on a good track. When you meet a road go left to arrive back in **Tong** village.

WHERE TO EAT AND DRINK ⓘ

You have a choice of pubs on this short walk. The **Greyhound**, in Tong, is a comfortable village inn with its own cricket pitch. The 17th-century building has beamed ceilings and a fine collection of antique toby jugs. Alternatively stop at the **Bankhouse Inn**, on the approach to the Moravian Settlement at Fulneck.

WHILE YOU'RE THERE ⓘ

Immediately over the M62 motorway you will find **Oakwell Hall**, dating from 1583. It is a splendid merchant clothier's house, built in the 'Halifax' style reminiscent of East Riddlesden Hall (► Walk 45). Remarkably, the interior of the house has undergone only minor changes, and retains many of its original Elizabethan features – not least the heavy oak panelling.

In Giant Rombald's Footsteps

A taste of West Yorkshire moorland from the village of Burley in Wharfedale.

•DISTANCE•	4 miles (6.4km)
•MINIMUM TIME•	2hrs
•ASCENT / GRADIENT•	560ft (170m) ▲▲▲
•LEVEL OF DIFFICULTY•	🚶🚶 🚶 🚶
•PATHS•	Good tracks and moorland paths, 5 stiles
•LANDSCAPE•	Moor and arable land
•SUGGESTED MAP•	aqua3 OS Explorer 297 Lower Wharfedale
•START / FINISH•	Grid reference: SE 163457
•DOG FRIENDLINESS•	Can be off lead but watch for grazing sheep
•PARKING•	Burley in Wharfedale Station car park
•PUBLIC TOILETS•	At railway station

BACKGROUND TO THE WALK

According to the legend, a giant by the name of Rombald used to live in these parts. While striding across the moor that now bears his name (in some versions of the story he was being chased by his angry wife) he dislodged a stone from a gritstone outcrop, and thus created the Calf, of the Cow and Calf rocks. Giants such as Rombald and Wade – and even the Devil himself – were apparently busy all over Yorkshire, dropping stones or creating big holes in the ground. It was perhaps an appealing way of accounting for some of the more unusual features of the landscape.

Rombalds Moor is pitted with old quarries, from which good quality stone was won. The Cow and Calf rocks used to be a complete family unit, but the rock known as the Bull was broken up to provide building stone.

The Hermit of Rombalds Moor

At Burley Woodhead a public house called the Hermit commemorates Job Senior, a local character with a chequered career. Job worked as a farm labourer, before succumbing to the demon drink. He met an elderly widow of independent means, who lived in a cottage at Coldstream Beck, on the edge of Rombalds Moor. Thinking he might get his hands on her money and home, Job married the old crone. Though she died soon after, Job took no profit. The family of her first husband pulled the cottage down, in Job's absence, leaving him homeless and penniless once more.

Enraged, he built himself a tiny hovel from the ruins of the house. Here he lived in filth and squalor on a diet of home-grown potatoes, which he roasted on a peat fire. He cut a strange figure, with a coat of multi-coloured patches and trousers held up with twine. He had long, lank hair, a matted beard and his legs were bandaged with straw. He made slow, rheumatic progress around Rombalds Moor with the aid of two crooked sticks.

His eccentric lifestyle soon had people flocking to see him. He offered weather predictions, and even advised visitors about their love lives. The possessor of a remarkable voice, he 'sang for his supper' as he lay on his bed of dried bracken and heather. These impromptu performances encouraged Job to sing in nearby villages, and even in the theatres of Leeds and Bradford. His speciality was sacred songs, which he would deliver

Walk 17

with great feeling. Nevertheless, his unwashed appearance meant that accommodation was never forthcoming, forcing him to bed down in barns or outhouses.

It was while staying in a barn that he was struck down with cholera. He was taken to Carlton Workhouse, where he died in 1857, aged 77. A huge crowd of people gathered at his funeral. Job Senior, the hermit of Rombalds Moor, was buried in the churchyard of Burley in Wharfedale. He's commorated in the old sign hanging over the entrance at the Hermit Inn.

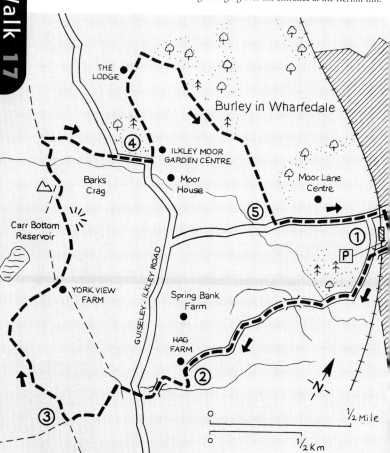

Walk 17 Directions

① From the station car park, cross the line via a footbridge and go left along a quiet lane. Follow the lane past houses and between fields up to **Hag Farm**.

② When the track wheels right, into the farmyard, keep left on a track to a stile and a gate.

Accompany a wall downhill; after 100yds (91m) take a gap stile in the wall. Bear off sharply to the right, to follow a stream up to another wall and gap stile. Follow a fence uphill to take another stile, cross the stream on a footbridge and join the approach road to a group of houses. Walk uphill to meet the **Guiseley–Ilkley road**. (To visit the **Hermit** pub you would need to go right here, for ¼ mile/400m.)

Walk 17

Cross the road and continue on a stony track ahead. After just 50yds (46m), ford a stream and follow a path uphill through woodland, onto a path hemmed in by hedges. Out onto open pasture you come to a gate. Follow the wall to your right, soon leaving it to take an indistinct path uphill.

③ Meet a stony track and follow it to the right, along the moorland edge. Follow a wall to a stile by a gate. Immediately after, keep right when the track forks. Keep right again as you approach a small brick building. Route-finding is now easy, as the track wheels around a farm. Keep left at the next farm (called **York View** because, on a clear day, you can see York Minster from here) to make a slow descent, following a wall on your right. As you approach a third farm, look out for two barns and a gate, on the right. Take an indistinct path to the left here, passing a small quarry. Enjoy level walking through bracken with great views over **Lower Wharfedale**. Go steeply

down a little ravine and cross a beck; continue up the other side. Before you reach the top, bear right and follow a path downhill to meet a road by a sharp bend.

④ Walk 100yds (91m) down the road, to another sharp right-hand bend. Bear left here (signed '**Ilkley Moor Garden Centre**'). Keep left of the garden centre itself, by continuing down the stony track. Keep left of a house, the **Lodge**; when the track bears sharp left towards a farm, your route is to the right, through a kissing gate, to follow a field path downhill with woodland to the left. After another kissing gate, follow a fence – then a wall – on the right. Beyond a third kissing gate and another gate, you join a tree-lined track heading to the right.

⑤ Meet a road and walk downhill back to the railway station car park.

WHAT TO LOOK FOR ℹ️
Rombalds Moor is home to the **red grouse**, often claimed to be the only truly indigenous British bird. Grouse take off from their heather hiding places with heart-stopping suddenness, with their evocative cry of 'go back, go back, go back'. Their moorland habitat is carefully managed to maintain a supply of young heather for the grouse to nest and feed in. This concern with their welfare has a commercial imperative. Grouse shooting is lucrative and the season begins on the 'Glorious Twelfth' of August.

Around Farnley Tyas

A delightful valley and views of Huddersfield's most prominent landmark.

•DISTANCE•	4½ miles (7.2km)
•MINIMUM TIME•	2hrs 30min
•ASCENT / GRADIENT•	360ft (110m) ▲▲▲
•LEVEL OF DIFFICULTY•	🚶 🚶 🚶
•PATHS•	Field paths, a little road walking on quiet lanes, 18 stiles
•LANDSCAPE•	Arable, rolling countryside and woodland
•SUGGESTED MAP•	aqua3 OS Explorer 288 Bradford & Huddersfield
•START / FINISH•	Grid reference: SE 162125
•DOG FRIENDLINESS•	Can be off lead but watch for traffic
•PARKING•	200yds (183m) up Butts Road by church in Farnley Tyas. Park in lay-by by recreation field
•PUBLIC TOILETS•	None on route

BACKGROUND TO THE WALK

Despite its proximity to Huddersfield, the area to the south of the town is surprisingly rural. As you gaze down into the Woodsome Valley from Farnley Tyas, you may feel a long way from the mills and terraced houses that typify the county. Farnley Tyas and the fortification of Castle Hill face each across the valley, and across the centuries. The village was mentioned in the Domesday Book, as 'Fereleia', but the history of Castle Hill extends at least 4,000 years. The site was inhabited by neolithic settlers who defended it with earth ramparts. Axe heads and other flint tools dating from this era have been found here during archaeological digs, and are now displayed in Huddersfield's Tolson Museum. The Stone Age settlers were just the first of many peoples who saw the hill's defensive potential. Its exposed position, with uninterrupted views on all sides, made it an ideal place for a fortification.

Almost 900 years ago the de Lacy family built a motte and bailey castle here, having been given land as a reward for their part in the Norman Conquest. Though the structure was demolished in the 14th century, the site has been known ever since as Castle Hill. Most of the earthworks and ramparts that can be seen today date from medieval times. To investigate them more closely, follow the extension detailed in Walk 19.

The name of Farnley Tyas, an attractive hill-top village, sounds rather posh for workaday West Yorkshire. Once plain Farnley, the village gained its double-barrelled moniker to differentiate it from other Farnleys – one near Leeds, the other near Otley. The 'Tyas' suffix is the name of the area's most prominent family, who owned land here from the 13th century onwards.

The Golden Cock

Originally a farm, the pub has been at the centre of village life – in every sense – since the 17th century. During the 19th century a group called the Royal Corkers used to ride over from Huddersfield to enjoy supper at the Golden Cock. Corks were placed on the dining table, with the last person to pick up a cork having to pay for supper for the whole party. Any newcomer to the group would naturally pick up a cork – but none of the regulars ever did – thus leaving the newcomer to pick up the bill.

Walk 18 Directions

① Enter the recreation field and follow the wall to your right. Squeeze past two gates, onto a walled track to meet a road. Go right (this is **Moor Lane**).

② 100yds (91m) past **Ivy Farm** bear right down a walled track, with **School Wood** to your right. You get views of **Castle Hill** ahead – a landmark you will see for most of this walk – and beyond to **Huddersfield**. To the left is **Meltham**, with the uplands of **Meltham Moor** behind. When the track bends right, towards **Ludhill Farm**, take a path on the left, between walls. Walk downhill to take a stile next to a metal gate, keeping left across a field, to another stile, and more steeply

Walk 18

downhill towards a few houses. Keep left at a fork of paths and walk between thick hedgerows, soon bearing left again to accompany a sunken path down to meet a road.

③ Go right, downhill. Bear right, after a small terrace of cottages, on a track into woodland. Bear left, after just 50yds (46m), on a lesser path that descends to a stile. Continue across a field (aim towards a farm ahead), cross a stream on stepping stones, then walk up through a spur of woodland. Cross the middle of another field, keeping to the left of **High Royd Farm**. Squeeze past a gate to join the farm's access track, walking uphill to meet a road by **High Royd Cottage**. Walk right, up the road, for 100yds (91m). Where the road bears right take a gap stile in the wall on your left by a gate. Follow a path between a wall and a fence; take another stile by a gate and bear right, uphill, along the field edge. Through a gap in a wall, cross another small field. Follow the edge of the next field, keeping a hedgerow to your left. The path levels out as **Castle Hill** comes into view again, and you meet a road.

④ Go right here, for just 20yds (18m), bearing left through a gap stile in the wall. Keep to the right of a short holly hedge, then follow a field-edge path, soon having a wall on your right. 150yds (138m) before you come to a wood, take a waymarked gap in the wall on your left. Follow the wall (now on your right) downhill, over a stile, and keep to the right-hand edge of the next field, with a little wooded valley on your right. Keep straight ahead at the next stile, now leaving the wood behind, but getting a sight of **Emley Moor** mast to your right.

Go through **Lumb Head** farmyard and join the access track to meet a road (Point Ⓐ on Walk 19). Go right here, downhill. After a couple of cottages, pass through a gap stile in a wall on the right.

⑤ Walk down into the valley, following the wall on your right. Take a stile and a few stone steps to cross a meandering stream, **Lumb Dike**, on a plank bridge, at a delectable woodland spot. Bear left, uphill, soon bearing left to follow the river, but at a higher level, through **Molly Carr Wood**. Descend to where two streams meet (you need to jump over this second beck). Follow the combined watercourse along the valley bottom and cross another side-beck. By taking a few paces to the right, uphill, you'll soon be able to join a more substantial track, through a gate and past a couple of houses, to come out at a road.

⑥ Go right, uphill (Point Ⓑ on Walk 19); 75yds (68m) past a sharp left-hand bend in the road, take a waymarked track sharply to the right, signed 'Farley Bank'. Pass a house; when the track bears right, to **Farnley Bank Farm**, take a stile ahead, and follow a field path uphill. Meet a road, and walk right, uphill, with good valley views all the way, back into **Farnley Tyas**. At a T-junction, by the **Golden Cock** pub, bear right, then left by the church on to **Butts Road** and return to your car.

WHERE TO EAT AND DRINK

The **Castle Hotel**, on top of Castle Hill, has an enviable position – enjoying panoramic views of the surrounding countryside. It's a popular place for a meal out; as is the **Golden Cock** in Farnley Tyas.

The View from Castle Hill

A stunning panorama, ancient earthworks and a Victorian folly that dominates the skyline.

See map and information panel for Walk 18

•DISTANCE•	5½ miles (8.8km)
•MINIMUM TIME•	3hrs
•ASCENT / GRADIENT•	690ft (210m) ▲▲▲
•LEVEL OF DIFFICULTY•	🚶🚶🚶

Walk 19 Directions (Walk 18 option)

Castle Hill is to the borough of Kirklees what Stoodley Pike is to Calderdale: a ubiquitous and much-loved landmark, visible for miles around. When the Norman castle was abandoned, during the 14th century, Castle Hill became a beacon site, one of a chain to warn of the Spanish Armada. During the 18th and 19th centuries Castle Hill was used for cock fighting, bull baiting and bare-knuckle fighting. Crowds gathered here for political rallies and religious meetings. The two buildings that can be seen today are modern additions to this historic site. The Castle Hill Hotel was built in 1852, and Jubilee Tower in 1898 to commemorate 60 years of Queen Victoria's reign. The tower rises 106ft (32m) above the hill's plateau, and dominates the skyline. On summer weekends you can climb the 165 steps inside and enjoy the spectacular panoramic views from the top.

From Point Ⓐ walk up the road, soon taking the narrow road, sharply on the right, that takes you up to the plateau of **Castle Hill**.

Having stopped to admire the view (expansive from every point of the compass), the tower, the earthworks – and perhaps calling in at the **Castle Hill Hotel** – walk right to join a sandy path, which is soon paved with stone. When the path forks keep straight on, now on a stony path downhill, with a fence to your left. Continue on this field-edge path, soon with a thorny hedgerow on the right. Join a stony track and continue downhill, along the field edge, over a stile, and approach a row of semi-detached houses. Take another stile and keep right of the last house, on a path, up to a road.

Go right, as the road becomes a track, going downhill, with woods to your left. Pass **Wheatroyd Lodge** on the left. Immediately before the next farm – **Wheatroyd Barn** – bear left by a fingerpost, through a gap in the fence. Join a path following a fence downhill with a wooded gully to your right. Weave your way down, between walls and fences, to approach a knot of houses. Go through a squeeze stile onto a concrete drive; follow this drive downhill to meet a quiet lane. Go left here, along **Lumb Lane,** to a T-junction. Bear sharp right, down **Sharp Lane**, to Point Ⓑ.

Walk 20

Bretton Hall & Country Park

A visit to a fine house, and an estate that's been transformed into an acclaimed sculpture park.

•DISTANCE•	4 miles (6.4km)
•MINIMUM TIME•	2hrs
•ASCENT / GRADIENT•	200ft (60m) ▲▲ ▲▲ ▲▲
•LEVEL OF DIFFICULTY•	林林 林 林
•PATHS•	Good paths and tracks all the way, 6 stiles
•LANDSCAPE•	Pasture, fields and parkland
•SUGGESTED MAP•	aqua3 OS Explorer 278 Sheffield & Barnsley
•START / FINISH•	Grid reference: SE 296124
•DOG FRIENDLINESS•	Leave dogs at home if you want to explore sculpture park
•PARKING•	Pay-and-display car park of Bretton Country Park, immediately off M1 at junction 38
•PUBLIC TOILETS•	At visitor centre adjacent to car park

Walk 20 Directions

Bretton Hall is a fine 18th-century mansion built by Sir William Wentworth, who was inspired, after going on a Grand Tour of Europe, to build in a grand Palladian style. He built his house on a hill, so that he could enjoy the view across the two lakes and landscaped parkland. Bretton Hall now has a new role as an educational campus, which has recently merged with the University of Leeds. In these tranquil surroundings, students can take degree courses in arts, music and performance.

> ### WHERE TO EAT AND DRINK ⓘ
> The **Bothy Café** in the sculpture park itself is your best bet for a sit down, a light snack and leisurely views of the artworks on display throughout the park. If you're seeking reliable pub food, try the **Black Bull** at Midgley, between West Bretton and Flockton. It's a Brewer's Fayre pub with a cosy atmosphere, and serves meals all day.

It may seem odd, at first, to find an outdoor sculpture park with an international reputation here in down-to-earth West Yorkshire. But with Henry Moore coming from Castleford, and Dame Barbara Hepworth from Wakefield, perhaps it's not so strange after all.

The sculpture park was established back in 1977, which makes it the first such venture in the United Kingdom. Exhibitions of modern and contemporary art are displayed in over 200 acres (81ha) of parkland, together with two galleries, providing a changing programme of exhibitions, displays and projects. Over 200,000 people a year visit this extraordinary 'art gallery without walls'.

In the adjacent Bretton Country Park is a collection of sculptures by Henry Moore. He was one of the first sculptors to create works for siting in informal landscape settings, where they would be encountered by people who were

WHAT TO LOOK FOR ⓘ

A number of **Henry Moore's sculptures** – monumental in scale, yet recognisably human – have found a permanent home at Bretton Park. Moore was born in nearby Castleford, began his artistic career at Leeds School of Art and remained close to his Yorkshire roots, even when his renown took on global proportions. He was a pioneer of outdoor sculpture, often creating works with particular landscape locations in mind. One of his most famous works sits on College Green, outside the Houses of Parliament in London. A version of his *Reclining Figure Draped* can be found outside the Civic Hall in Castleford, and there is a *Reclining Figure* from 1936 in Wakefield Museum.

unlikely to visit a gallery. So it seems fitting that a dozen of Moore's monumental bronze figures have found a permanent home here. Both the Yorkshire Sculpture Park and Bretton Country Park are open all year round, and entrance is free.

Rejoin the road and walk right for 200yds (182m), then take **Jebb Lane** to the right. Pass a few cottages, soon bearing right in front of a large barn onto a stony track (signed to **Bretton Park**). Go through a gate, onto an obvious field path. The path bears left, around woodland. Cross a stile in a fence and follow the fence to the right, towards another wood. Bear left, to follow the field-edge path, with woodland on your right. At the top of the hill cross two stiles in quick succession.

Continue walking in the same direction, now following a footpath downhill through pleasant pasture land. Where a track goes off to the right, at a small pond, your route is to the left, on a lesser path going

uphill, between fields. Cross a stile and continue uphill across a field. At the next fence you meet an obvious stony track.

Follow the track and the fence to the right, downhill, getting good views of **Bretton Hall**. When the track bears right, go through a gate in decorative stone gateposts ahead. Cross a bridge that divides a lake in two, and continue through another gate. When your track bears right, keep on a lesser track ahead, slightly uphill. The track wheels right, at the top, bringing you to the main entrance of the sculpture park.

Take time to look at the sculptures, which are spread throughout the park. There are two smaller galleries – the **Bothy Gallery** and **Pavilion Gallery** – plus the **Bothy Café**. Walk gradually downhill until you reach the **River Dearne**.

Follow the river to the left, through a gate and into **Bretton Country Park** again. Walk through parkland, passing an elaborate, arched bridge and a cascade of weirs. The path soon leads you back to the visitor centre and car park.

WHILE YOU'RE THERE ⓘ

Take a trip to the **National Coal Mining Museum for England**, on the A642 half-way between Wakefield and Huddersfield. When the coal seams at the Caphouse Colliery were exhausted, during the mid-1980s, the site was converted into a museum. Visitors can explore the oldest coal mine shaft still in everyday use in Britain today, and learn about an industry which already seems to belong to our nation's past. Local miners are now guides through the workings, taking you 450ft (137m) below ground. There are also pit ponies, rides on the miners' train and a licensed café and shop.

A Taste of the Last of the Summer Wine

Follow in the footsteps of the immortal Compo, Foggy and Clegg on their South Pennine adventures.

•DISTANCE•	4½ miles (7.2km)
•MINIMUM TIME•	2hrs
•ASCENT / GRADIENT•	558ft (170m) ▲ ▲ ▲
•LEVEL OF DIFFICULTY•	🚶 🚶 🚶
•PATHS•	Good paths and tracks, 8 stiles
•LANDSCAPE•	Upland pasture
•SUGGESTED MAP•	aqua3 OS Explorer 288 Bradford & Huddersfield
•START / FINISH•	Grid reference: SE 143084
•DOG FRIENDLINESS•	Can be off lead except in central Holmfirth
•PARKING•	Centre of Holmfirth gets very crowded, so park in Crown Bottom car park (pay-and-display) on Huddersfield Road
•PUBLIC TOILETS•	Holmfirth

BACKGROUND TO THE WALK

Holmfirth and the Holme Valley have been popularised as 'Summer Wine Country'. The whimsical TV series, starring the trio of incorrigible old buffers Compo, Foggy and Clegg, has now been running for a quarter of a century. These larger-than-life characters, going back to their second childhoods, have proved to be an irresistible formula in the hands of writer Roy Clarke.

Last of the Summer Wine was first seen in January 1973, as a one-off Comedy Playhouse episode. The response was so good that a six-part series was commissioned. The rest is history, with *Summer Wine* becoming the UK's longest running comedy programme.

The cast have become familiar faces around Holmfirth. So much so that when Londoner Bill Owen (lovable rogue 'Compo') died in 1999 at the age of 85, he was laid to rest overlooking the little town he had grown to call home. As a sign that this affection is reciprocated, there are plans afoot to erect a statue of Compo in the town. With Bill Owen's son Tom having joined the cast, who knows; perhaps the series has plenty of life in it yet.

Visitors come to Holmfirth in droves, in search of film locations such as Sid's Café and Nora Batty's house. But Holmfirth takes TV fame in its stride, for this isn't the first time that the town has starred in front of the cameras. In fact, Holmfirth very nearly became another Hollywood. Bamforths – better known for its naughty seaside postcards – began to make short films here in the early years of the last century. They were exported around the world. Local people were drafted in as extras in Bamforth's overwrought dramas. Film production came to an end at the outbreak of the First World War and, sadly, was never resumed.

Holmfirth

Holmfirth town, much more than just a film set, is the real star – along with the stunning South Pennine scenery which surrounds it. By the time you have completed half of this walk, you are but a mile (1.6km) from the Peak National Park.

The town grew rapidly with the textile trades, creating a tight-knit community in the valley bottom: a maze of ginnels, alleyways and narrow lanes. The River Holme, which runs through its middle, has flooded on many occasions. But the most devastating flood occurred back in 1852 when, after heavy rain, Bilberry Reservoir burst its banks. The resulting torrent of water destroyed the centre of Holmfirth and claimed 81 lives. The tragedy was reported at length on the front page of the *London Illustrated News*, complete with an artist's impression of the devastation. A public subscription fund was started to help the flood survivors to rebuild the town. These traumatic events are marked by a monument near the bus station.

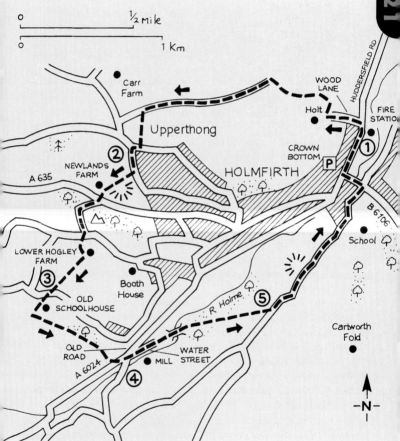

Walk 21 Directions

① From **Crown Bottom** car park, walk to the right along **Huddersfield Road** for just 100yds (91m) before bearing left opposite the fire station, up **Wood Lane**. The road soon narrows to a steep track.

Keep left of a house and through a gate, to continue on a walled path. At the top of the hill, by a bench, follow the track to the right. Follow this track, soon enclosed, as it wheels left, down into a valley. Soon after you approach woodland, you have a choice of tracks: keep left on the walled path, uphill.

Join a more substantial farm track and, 100yds (91m) before the cottage ahead, look for a wall stile on the left. Follow a field path to emerge, between houses, in the village of **Upperthong**.

② Bear left along the road, which wheels round to the right. Walk downhill, with great views opening up of the **Holme Valley**. After 150yds (138m) on the road, take a cinder track on the right. Walk down past **Newlands Farm** to meet a road. Cross over and take the lane ahead, steeply down into a little valley and up the other side. When this minor road forks at the top, go right, uphill. Immediately after the first house, go left, on a sandy track. Follow this track to **Lower Hogley Farm** where you keep right, past a knot of houses, to a gate and on to a field path, with a wall to your left. Over a stile, cross the next field, now with the wall to your right. Past the next wall stile, veer half left across the next field (aim for the mast on the horizon). After one more field, descend to a road.

③ Go right for just 50yds (46m) to bear left around an old schoolhouse on a grassy path. Follow the walled path downhill, through a gate; as the path opens out into a grassy area, bear left on a grassy track down into the valley. Follow a high

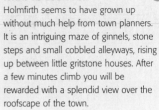

WHAT TO LOOK FOR

Holmfirth seems to have grown up without much help from town planners. It is an intriguing maze of ginnels, stone steps and small cobbled alleyways, rising up between little gritstone houses. After a few minutes climb you will be rewarded with a splendid view over the roofscape of the town.

wall on your right, over a stile, on to an enclosed path. On approaching houses, take a stile and join a metalled track at a fork. Bear right here, then immediately left, on a narrow path between houses. Follow a field path through a gate; pass houses and a mill down to meet the main A6024 road.

④ Cross the road; by a row of diminutive cottages take **Old Road** to the left. Keep straight ahead at a junction down **Water Street**. Beyond a mill, cross the **River Holme** on a metal footbridge and follow a riverside path. Soon the path veers right through pasture; when the path forks, keep right, uphill, to enter woodland. Continue in the same direction, uphill, emerging from the wood on to a field path. After two stiles join a track by a house. Pass more cottages to meet a road.

⑤ Go left, along the road. You should enjoy splendid views down into the **Holme Valley** below you, as you make the long descent back into **Holmfirth**.

WHILE YOU'RE THERE

If you continue to drive through Holmfirth on the A6024, you pass Holmbridge, then Holme, before the Holme Valley comes to a dramatic end, surrounded by a huge sweep of rugged moorland. As you climb steeply to the height of Holme Moss, topped with a TV mast, you enter the Peak National Park.

WHERE TO EAT AND DRINK

With so many visitors, Holmfirth is well supplied with pubs and tea shops. **Compo's Café**, smack in the centre of town, will already be familiar to fans of *Last of the Summer Wine*.

Along the Wharfe to a Victorian Spa Town

From Addingham to Ilkley, along a stretch of the lovely River Wharfe.

•DISTANCE•	5½ miles (8.8km)
•MINIMUM TIME•	2hrs 30min
•ASCENT / GRADIENT•	197ft (60m) ▲▲ ▲
•LEVEL OF DIFFICULTY•	🚶 🚶 🚶
•PATHS•	Riverside path and field paths, some road walking, 7 stiles
•LANDSCAPE•	Rolling country and the River Wharfe
•SUGGESTED MAP•	aqua3 OS Explorer 297 Lower Wharfedale
•START / FINISH•	Grid reference: SE 084498
•DOG FRIENDLINESS•	Keep on lead on minor roads
•PARKING•	Lay-by at eastern end of Addingham, on bend where North Street becomes Bark Lane by information panel
•PUBLIC TOILETS•	Ilkley

BACKGROUND TO THE WALK

Addingham is not one of those compact Yorkshire villages that huddles around a village green. The houses extend for a mile (1.6km) on either side of the main street, with St Peter's Church at the eastern end of the village, close to the river. So it's no surprise that the village used to known as 'Long Addingham', and that it is actually an amalgamation of three separate communities that grew as the textile trades expanded. Having been by-passed in recent years, Addingham is now a quiet backwater.

Within 50 years, from the end of the 17th century, Addingham's population quadrupled, from 500 to 2,000. Even here, at the gateway to the Yorkshire Dales, the textile industries flourished. At the height of the boom, there were six woollen mills in the village. Low Mill, built in 1787, was the scene of a riot by a band of Luddites – weavers and shearers who objected to their jobs being done by machines. Though the mill itself was demolished in 1972, more houses were added to the mill-hands' cottages to create Low Mill Village, a pleasant riverside community.

Ilkley

Visitors from, say, Bath or Cheltenham should feel quite at home in Ilkley, a town that seems to have more in common with Harrogate, its even posher neighbour to the north, than with the textile towns of West Yorkshire. The Romans established an important fort here – believed to be 'Olicana' – on a site close to where the parish church is today. Two Roman altars were incorporated into the base of the church tower, and in the churchyard can be found three Anglo-Saxon crosses that date back to the 9th century. One of the few tangible remains of the Roman settlement is a short stretch of wall near the handsome Manor House, which is now a museum.

Like nearby Harrogate, Ilkley's fortunes changed dramatically with the discovery of medicinal springs. During the reign of Queen Victoria, the great and the good would come here to 'take the waters' and socialise at the town's hydros and hotels. Visitor numbers increased with the coming of the railway, and included such luminaries as Madame Tussaud, George Bernard Shaw and Charles Darwin, taking a well-earned rest after the publication of the *Origin of Species*.

With its open-air swimming pool and riverside promenades, Ilkley was almost an inland resort. Though we have replaced water cures with more sophisticated quackery, Ilkley remains a prosperous town, unashamedly dedicated to the good things of life.

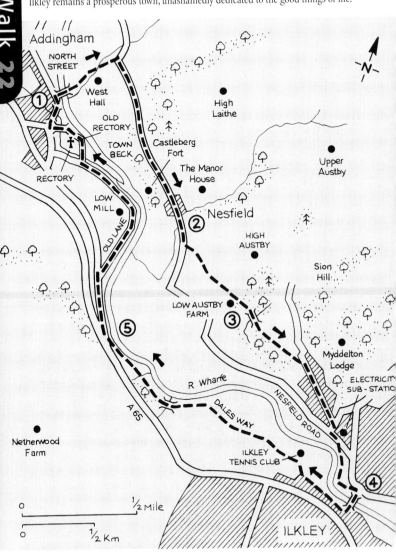

Walk 22 Directions

① Walk 50yds (46m) up the road, and take stone steps down to the right, (signed '**Dales Way**'). Bear

immediately right again, and cross the **River Wharfe** on a suspension bridge. Follow a metalled path along a field edge. Cross a stream and join a metalled track between walls that soon emerges at a minor

WHERE TO EAT AND DRINK ℹ️

In Addingham try the **Sailor's Arms** or the **Fleece** for traditional pub food. At the bottom end of Ilkley you are close to the **'The Taps'** or the Ilkley Moor Vaults as it officially called, and the **Riverside Hotel**, which is particularly child-friendly.

road by a sharp bend. Go right here; after about ½ mile (800m) of road walking you reach the little community of **Nesfield**.

② About 100yds (91m) beyond the last house, and immediately after the road crosses a stream, bear left up a stony track (signed as a footpath to **High Austby**). Immediately take a stile between two gates. Cross the field ahead, keeping parallel to the road (ignoring a track going left, uphill). There is no obvious path; follow the wall on your right, over a stile. Beyond a small conifer plantation, take a ladder stile in the fence ahead to keep left of **Low Austby Farm**.

③ Cross a footbridge over a stream; beyond a stile you enter woodland. Follow a path downhill, leaving the wood by another step stile. Follow a fence uphill, then cross the middle of a field to locate a stile at the far end, to enter more woodland. Follow an obvious path through the trees, before reaching a road via a wall stile. Go right, downhill, to reach a road junction. Go right again, crossing **Nesfield Road**, and take a path to the left of an electricity sub-station. You have a few minutes of riverside walking before you reach Ilkley's old stone bridge.

④ Cross the bridge. This is your opportunity to explore the spa town of **Ilkley**. Otherwise you should turn right, immediately after the

bridge, on to a riverside path (from here back to **Addingham** you are following the well-signed **Dales Way**). You soon continue along a lane, passing **Ilkley Tennis Club**. Opposite the clubhouse, take a footpath to the left, through a kissing gate, and across pasture. You have seven more kissing gates to negotiate before you are back by the **River Wharfe** again. Cross a stream on a footbridge, and enter woodland. Cross another stream to meet a stony track. Go right, downhill, on this track to the river. Through another kissing gate, you follow a grassy path (with woodland and a fence to your left) before joining the old A65 road. Thanks to the by-pass it is now almost empty of traffic.

⑤ Follow the road by the riverside. After almost ½ mile (800m) of road walking, go right, just before a row of terraced houses, on to **Old Lane**. Pass between the houses of a new development – **Low Mill Village** – to locate a riverside path, now metalled, at the far side. Once you have passed the Rectory on the left, and the grounds of the **Old Rectory** on your right, look for a kissing gate on the right. Take steps and follow the path to a tiny arched bridge over **Town Beck**. You have a grassy path across pasture, in front of the church, before taking another bridge, between houses, to re-emerge on **North Street** in **Addingham**.

WHILE YOU'RE THERE ℹ️

Addingham lies at the north western edge of the county. Just a mile to the north you enter the Yorkshire Dales National Park. By following the B6160 you soon come to **Bolton Abbey**, with its priory ruins in an idyllic setting by a bend in the River Wharfe.

Shipley Glen's Tramway and Baildon Moor

A glimpse of moorland and a traditional rural playground for the mill workers of Shipley and Saltaire.

•DISTANCE•	4 miles (6.4km)
•MINIMUM TIME•	2hrs
•ASCENT / GRADIENT•	492ft (150m) ▲▲ ▲
•LEVEL OF DIFFICULTY•	🚶🚶 🚶🚶 🚶🚶
•PATHS•	Moor and field paths, 1 stile
•LANDSCAPE•	Moorland, fields and gritstone rocks
•SUGGESTED MAP•	aqua3 OS Explorer 288 Bradford & Huddersfield
•START / FINISH•	Grid reference: SE 132389
•DOG FRIENDLINESS•	Can be off leads except in Saltaire
•PARKING•	On Glen Road, between Bracken Hall Countryside Centre and Old Glen House pub
•PUBLIC TOILETS•	At Bracken Hall Countryside Centre; also near Old Glen House pub and in Saltaire

BACKGROUND TO THE WALK

For the people of Shipley and Saltaire, Baildon Moor has traditionally represented a taste of the countryside on their doorsteps. Mill-hands could leave the mills and cramped terraced streets behind, and breathe clean Pennine air. They could listen to the song of the skylark and the bubbling cry of the curlew. There were heather moors to tramp across, gritstone rocks to scramble up and, at Shipley Glen, springy sheep-grazed turf on which to spread out a picnic blanket. There was also a funfair to visit – not a little funfair, like there still is today – but a veritable theme park.

Towards the end of the 19th century Shipley Glen was owned by a Colonel Maude, who created a number of attractions. Visitors could enjoy the sundry delights of the Switchback Railway, Marsden's Menagerie, the Horse Tramway and the Aerial Runway. More sedate pleasures could be found at the Camera Obscura, the boating lake in the Japanese garden, and the Temperance Tea Room and Coffee House.

Sam Wilson, a local entrepreneur, played his own part in developing Shipley Glen. In 1895 he created the Shipley Glen Tramway. Saltaire people could now stroll through Roberts Park, past the steely-gazed statue of Sir Titus Salt, and enjoy the tram-ride to the top of the glen. Thousands of people would clamber, each weekend, on to the little cable-hauled 'toast-rack' cars. As one car went up the hill, another car would descend on an adjacent track.

In commercial terms, the heyday of Shipley Glen was during the Edwardian era. On busy days as many as 17,000 people would take the tramway up to the pleasure gardens. Losing out to more sophisticated entertainments, however, Shipley Glen went into a slow decline. Most of the attractions are now gone, but not all. You can still ride the Aerial Runway (though it's not exactly a white-knuckle ride) and spend some money at the little funfair. Best of all, you can still take the tramway – which runs every day from May to September, with more restrictive operation during the winter.

The Old Glen House is still a popular pub, though the Temperance Tea Room and Coffee House have been transformed into the Bracken Hall Countryside Centre. Local people still enjoy the freedom of the heather moorland. Despite all the changes, Shipley Glen retains a stubbornly old-fashioned air, and is all the better for it.

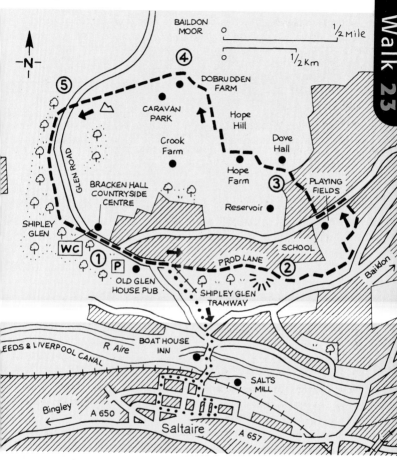

Walk 23 Directions

① Walk down **Glen Road**, passing the **Old Glen House** pub. Continue as the road becomes **Prod Lane**, signed as a cul-de-sac. Pass the tiny funfair and the entrance to the **Shipley Glen Tramway**. Where the road ends, keep straight ahead to locate an enclosed path to the right of a house. Follow this path, with houses on your left, and woodland to your right. As you come to a

metal barrier, ignore a path to the left. Keep straight on downhill. 100yds (91m) beyond the barrier, you have a choice of paths; bear left here, uphill, soon getting good views over **Saltaire**, **Shipley** and the **Aire Valley**.

② Beyond the woodland, you walk beneath a quarried sandstone cliff. When you come to an open area, with panoramic views, take a set of stone steps, with metal handrails, up to the top of the cliff. Bear right

Walk 23

on a path between chain-link fences, which takes you around school playing fields, to meet a road. Walk left along the road for 150yds (138m). When you are level with the school on your left, cross the road and take a narrow, enclosed path on the right, between houses. Walk gradually uphill, crossing a road in a housing estate and picking up the enclosed path again. Soon, at a stile, you emerge into pasture.

③ Go half left, uphill, to a kissing gate at the top-left corner of the field. Before you reach the farm you see ahead, join the access track, walking past the buildings on a cinder track till a metal gate bars your way. Go right here, through a wooden gate, on a path between walls. Beyond the next gate you come out on to **Baildon Moor**.

Your path is clear, following a wall to your left. Keep straight on, as the wall curves to the left, towards the next farm (and caravan park). Cross a metalled farm track and curve left to follow the boundary wall of **Dobrudden Farm**.

④ Walk gradually downhill towards **Bingley** in the valley. When the wall bears left, keep straight ahead, through bracken, more steeply downhill. Cross a metalled track and carry on down to meet **Glen Road** again.

⑤ Follow the path along the rocky edge of wooded **Shipley Glen** leading you back to the **Bracken Hall Countryside Centre** and your car.

The Town Sir Titus Built

Walk the streets of Saltaire, a model village built for the workers at Salts Mill.
See map and information panel for Walk 23

•DISTANCE•	1½ miles (2.4km)
•MINIMUM TIME•	2hrs
•ASCENT / GRADIENT•	130ft (40m) ▲ ▲ ▲
•LEVEL OF DIFFICULTY•	🚶 🚶 🚶

Walk 24 Directions
(Walk 23 option)

There's so much to see in Shipley Glen and Saltaire. Do Walk 23 in the morning, take the tramway down into the valley and have lunch at the Boathouse Inn. Leave the afternoon to explore Salt's Mill and the model village of Saltaire.

Walk back down **Glen Road** to the upper terminus of the **Shipley Glen Tramway** and take the easy way down into the valley (or, if the tramway is not running, follow the adjacent path). At the bottom of the hill is a small museum devoted to the chequered history of the tramway. Continue down the path into **Roberts Park**, where a statue of Sir Titus Salt still stands. At the far end of the park a footbridge crosses the **River Aire** (and gives access to the **Boathouse Inn**). Cross the **Leeds and Liverpool Canal**, then the railway line, into **Saltaire** itself. After a leisurely exploration of Titus Salt's model village, retrace your steps – and take the tramway – back up to **Shipley Glen**.

Saltaire's founding father was Sir Titus Salt, a Victorian industrialist and patriarch, who already owned six textile mills in Bradford. He made a considerable fortune from spinning alpaca fleece and, seeing the smoky, Dickensian squalor of life in the city, decided to build a new settlement for his employees.

Sir Titus designed Saltaire as a community where his mill workers could live in clean, sanitary conditions. Begun in 1851, it was 20 years in the making. As a contrast to many areas of Bradford, even the most modest dwelling in Saltaire had gas, running water and a toilet. In his plan Sir Titus included schools, a bathhouse, laundry, hospital and a row of almshouses. A workers' dining room could seat 800. The neat streets of terraced houses were named after the founder (Titus Street), his wife, Caroline, and children... not forgetting the reigning monarch (Victoria Street) and her consort (Albert Road).

The centrepiece of his scheme was Salts Mill, a monumental example of industrial architecture which straddles the Leeds and Liverpool Canal. The chimney is a copy of the bell tower of a church in Venice. In recent years the mill has enjoyed a new lease of life as a showcase for the artworks of David Hockney, who was born in Bradford.

Walk 25

Surprise View and Otley Chevin

Enjoy woodland walks and panoramic views across the Wharfe Valley.

•DISTANCE•	3 miles (4.8km)
•MINIMUM TIME•	1hr 30min
•ASCENT / GRADIENT•	328ft (100m) ▲
•LEVEL OF DIFFICULTY•	🚶🚶
•PATHS•	Easy walking on good paths and forestry tracks, no stiles
•LANDSCAPE•	Heath and woodland
•SUGGESTED MAP•	aqua3 OS Explorer 297 Lower Wharfedale
•START / FINISH•	Grid reference: SE 205431
•DOG FRIENDLINESS•	Dogs can run free all over the Chevin
•PARKING•	Beacon House car park on Yorkgate, opposite Royalty Inn
•PUBLIC TOILETS•	None on route

Walk 25 Directions

This walk begins at **Surprise View** and, if this is your first visit, you will have a surprise indeed. By strolling just a few paces from your car you can enjoy a breathtaking panorama across Lower Wharfedale. Almscliffe Crag is a prominent landmark in the valley. On a clear day, you may be able to see Simon's Seat, and even the famous White Horse carved into the hillside at Kilburn. With so much to see, it's easy to forget that you are only a mile (1.6km) away from the bustle of the Leeds–Bradford Airport.

The Chevin has traditionally been a popular destination for walkers and picnickers. In 1944 Major Fawkes of Farnley Hall gave a piece of land on the Chevin to the people of Otley. By 1989, when it was designated a local nature reserve, the Chevin Forest Park had grown to 700 acres (283ha) of woodland, heath and gritstone crags. Local people come here to walk their dogs, and the broad forest tracks are ideal for horse riders and mountain bikers. The walk featured here is merely one – short – possibility; the park is criss-crossed by good waymarked paths.

Immediately below the Chevin is the market town of Otley, straddling the River Wharfe, and well worth visiting in its own right. Wharfemeadows Park offers riverside strolls and rowing boats for hire. Thomas Chippendale, the famous furniture maker, was born in Otley in 1710.

Otley was granted its market charter back in 1222, and the cobbled market square still occupies the centre of town. On market days (Fridays and Saturdays) the stalls overflow along the main street of Kirkgate. There are weekly livestock markets too and Otley Show, each spring, is a big date in the local calendar. The Otley Folk Festival attracts music lovers every autumn; over a long weekend you can hardly move for mummers and morris dancers. Otley is famous – or perhaps infamous – for having more pubs per head of population than anywhere else in Yorkshire. Even though a by-pass now keeps a lot of traffic away, it's still a busy little town.

From the far end of the car park you have access to the **Chevin Ridge**, with its splendid birds-eye view of **Otley** and **Lower Wharfedale**. Join the obvious path, going to the right, which is also a section of the **Dales Way**. Follow the wall on your right, walking gradually downhill and through a gate. Keep left, still downhill, on a track which descends to meet a road by a house (**Danefield House**). Walk right, up the road, for about 200yds (183m) to reach another car park.

Go left here, to a fork of good forestry tracks by an information board. Take the right-hand option, to enjoy easy walking on a sandy track through, predominantly conifer woodland. Beyond a little bridge, keep left at another choice of tracks. As you leave the woods you come to a meeting of tracks, with a gate and kissing gate on the left. Go through the kissing gate and keep left on a path that soon rewards you with a view over the valley, and **Caley Crags** – popular with novice climbers – immediately below you.

Keep left, to walk through mixed woodland. Go through a kissing gate and continue on a good sandy track. Where the track forks keep left, descending to cross a beck on a wooden footbridge. Follow the track uphill, to the car park. From here you retrace your steps, that is: go right, down the road for 200yds (183m), and bear left by **Danefield House**. Follow the track uphill, then bear right, squeezing past a gate, to rejoin the ridge-top track. Soon you are back at **Surprise View**; take a last look at that inspiring view before you find your car, or enjoy a drink at the nearby **Royalty Inn**.

Halifax and the Shibden Valley

An old packhorse track, a superb half-timbered hall and a hidden valley – all just a short walk from Halifax.

•DISTANCE•	4½ miles (7.2km)
•MINIMUM TIME•	2hrs 30min
•ASCENT / GRADIENT•	410ft (125m) ▲▲
•LEVEL OF DIFFICULTY•	🚶 🚶 🚶
•PATHS•	Old packhorse tracks and field paths, no stiles
•LANDSCAPE•	Surprisingly rural, considering the proximity to Halifax
•SUGGESTED MAP•	aqua3 OS Explorer 288 Bradford & Huddersfield
•START / FINISH•	Grid reference: SE 095254
•DOG FRIENDLINESS•	Keep on lead crossing busy roads
•PARKING•	In Halifax
•PUBLIC TOILETS•	Halifax (near bus station)

BACKGROUND TO THE WALK

Set amongst the Pennine hills, Halifax was a town in the vanguard of the Industrial Revolution. Its splendid civic buildings and huge mills are a good indication of the town's prosperity, won from the woollen trade. Ironically, the most splendid building of all came close to being demolished. The Piece Hall, built in 1779, predates the industrial era. Here, in a total of 315 rooms on three collonaded floors, the hand-weavers of the district would offer their wares (known as 'pieces') for sale to cloth merchants. The collonades surround a massive square. Your first reaction on walking into the square may be surprise, for this is a building that would not look out of place in Renaissance Italy.

The mechanisation of the weaving process left the Piece Hall largely redundant. In the intervening years it has served a variety of purposes, including as a venue for political oration and as a wholesale market. During the 1970s, having narrowly escaped the wrecking ball, the Piece Hall was spruced up and given a new lease of life. Now it houses a museum, tourist information centre and a number of small shops and businesses. But the buildings full potential as a tourist attraction has yet to be realised.

The Magna Via

The cobbled thoroughfare that climbs so steeply up Beacon Hill is known as the Magna Via. Until 1741, when a turnpike road was built, this was the only practicable approach to Halifax from the east, for both foot and packhorse traffic. Also known as Wakefield Gate, the Magna Via linked up with the Long Causeway, the old high level road to Burnley. That intrepid 18th-century traveller, Daniel Defoe, was one of those who struggled up this hill. 'We quitted Halifax not without some astonishment at its situation, being so surrounded with hills, and those so high as makes the coming in and going out of it exceedingly troublesome'. The route was superseded in the 1820s by the turnpike constructed through Godley Cutting. Today the Magna Via, too steep to be adopted for modern motor vehicles, remains a fascinating relic of the past.

Shibden Hall

Situated on a hill above Halifax, this magnificent half-timbered house is set in 90 acres (36ha) of beautiful, rolling parkland. Dating from 1420, the hall has been owned by prominent local families – the Oates, Saviles, Waterhouses and, latterly, the Listers. All these families left their mark on the fabric of the house, but, the core of the original house remains intact. The rooms are furnished in period style, to show how they might have looked over almost six centuries. The oak furniture and panelling has that patina of age that antique forgers try in vain to emulate. Barns and other outbuildings have been converted into a folk museum, with displays of old vehicles, tools and farm machinery.

When Emily Brontë created Thrushcross Grange in her only novel *Wuthering Heights*, she may have had Shibden Hall in mind. It certainly proved a suitable location in 1991 for a new film version of the famous story, which starred Ralph Fiennes as Heathcliffe and Juliette Binoche as Cathy.

Walk 26 Directions

① Walk downhill, past a tall spire that once belonged to **Square Church**, and down **Church Street**, passing the smoke-blackened parish church. Bear left on to **Lower Kirkgate**, then right on to **Bank Bottom**. Cross **Hebble Brook** and

Walk 26

walk uphill; where the road bears sharp left, keep straight ahead up a steep cobbled lane. When you meet a road, go right for about 200yds (183m). Just after the entrance to a warehouse (Aquaspersion), take a cobbled path on the left that makes a steep ascent up **Beacon Hill**.

② This old packhorse track – known as the **Magna Via** – joins another path and continues uphill to a large retaining wall, where you have a choice of tracks. Keep left on a cinder track, slightly downhill, as views open up of the surprisingly rural **Shibden Valley**. Keep left when the track forks again; after a further 100yds (91m) take a walled path on the left (signed to **Stump Cross**). Follow a hedgerow downhill through a little estate of new houses to a road. Cross here and take a gated path immediately to the right of a farm entrance, which takes you downhill, under the railway line and into **Shibden Park**, close to the boating lake.

③ Follow a drive uphill. Near the top of the hill you will find a footpath on the left, giving access to the Elizabethan splendour of **Shibden Hall** itself. Otherwise, continue uphill; just before you meet the main A58 road, bear right, down **Old Godley Lane**. Pass houses and take steps up to the main road at the busy junction of **Stump Cross**.

④ Cross over the road and take **Staups Lane**, to the left of the **Stump Cross Inn**. Walk up the lane, which soon becomes cobbled, to meet another surfaced road. Bear left here, down a metalled track, through a gate, to join a straight, double-paved track into **Shibden Dale**. When the paving ends, continue via a gate and through open pasture. Turn left, at the next gate, walking down a lane that soon leads you to the **Shibden Mill Inn**.

⑤ Walk to the far end of the pub's car park, to join a track that crosses **Shibden Beck**. Beyond a brick-built house, the track narrows to a walled path. You emerge from countryside, to walk past the houses of **Claremont** and cross the main A58 road, as it goes through the steep-sided **Godley Cutting**, on a bridge. Take a set of steps immediately after the bridge and walk left along the road. From here you can retrace your route of earlier in the day, back into **Halifax**.

Walk 27

A Colourful Circuit of Norland Moor

Awash with colour in late summer, Norland Moor is an island of heather moorland in the midst of busy milltowns.

•DISTANCE•	5 miles (8km)
•MINIMUM TIME•	2hrs 30min
•ASCENT / GRADIENT•	328ft (100m)
•LEVEL OF DIFFICULTY•	
•PATHS•	Good moorland paths and tracks, 1 stile
•LANDSCAPE•	Heather moor and woodland
•SUGGESTED MAP•	aqua3 OS Outdoor Leisure 21 South Pennines
•START / FINISH•	Grid reference: SE 055218
•DOG FRIENDLINESS•	Dogs can roam off lead, though watch for grazing sheep
•PARKING•	Small public car park opposite Moorcock Inn, on unclassified road immediately south of Sowerby Bridge
•PUBLIC TOILETS•	None on route

BACKGROUND TO THE WALK

Norland Moor and North Dean Woods are close to the start of the Calderdale Way, a 50-mile (80-km) circuit of the borough of Calderdale. There are panoramic views straight away, as the waymarked walk accompanies the edge of Norland Moor. The route was inaugurated during the 1970s to link some of the best Pennine landscapes and historical sites – moors, mills, gritstone outcrops, wooded cloughs, hand-weaving hamlets and industrial towns – into an invigorating walk.

Norland Moor

Norland Moor is a 253-acre (102-ha) tract of heather moorland overlooking Sowerby Bridge and both the Calder and Ryburn valleys. Criss-crossed by paths, it is popular with local walkers; riven by old quarry workings, it is a reminder that here in West Yorkshire you are seldom far from a site of industry. Originally a part of the Savile estates, the moor was bought for £250 after a public appeal in 1932. It still has the status of a common. Part of the attraction is to find such splendid walking country so close to the busy towns in the valley.

Ladstone Rock is a gritstone outcrop with a distinctive profile that stares out over the Ryburn Valley from the edge of Norland Moor. If you can believe the stories, human sacrifices were carried out on Ladstone Rock by blood-thirsty druids, and convicted witches were thrown off it. The name may derive from Celtic roots, meaning to cut or to kill. There is a tradition in the South Pennines of carving inspirational quotations into such rocks. And here on Ladstone Rock, amongst the names, dates and expressions of undying love, is a small metal plaque inscribed with a short psalm from the Bible.

Wainhouse Tower

As you leave the nature reserve of North Dean Woods behind, you get good views across the valley to Sowerby Bridge and the outskirts of Halifax. Dominating the view is a curious edifice known as Wainhouse Tower (and also, tellingly, as Wainhouse Folly). It was built by John Wainhouse, who had inherited his uncle's dyeworks. His first plan was to build a tall chimney that would help to disperse the noxious fumes from the dyeworks. But then he decided to add a spiral staircase, inside the chimney, leading up to an ornate viewing platform at the top. By the time the tower was actually built, in the 1870s, the original purpose seems to have been forgotten. To climb to the full height of the tower, 253 ft (77m), you need to tackle more than 400 steps. The tower is opened up to the public, but on just a few occasions each year – generally on bank holidays. If Wainhouse failed to make a chimney, then he succeeded in creating a distinctive landmark.

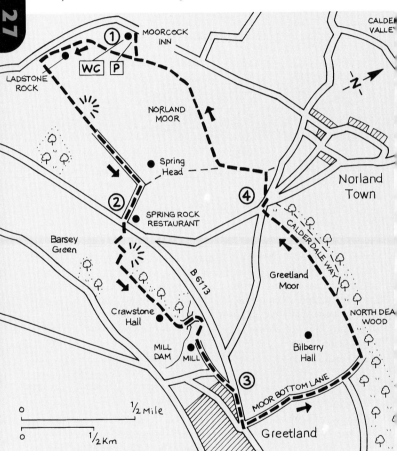

Walk 27 Directions

① Walk uphill from the **Moorcock Inn**, bearing right near the top to follow a clear path along the edge of **Norland Moor**. Enjoy expansive views across the **Calder Valley** as you pass the gritstone outcrop known as **Ladstone Rock**. Keep straight ahead, now on a more substantial track which descends almost to a road. Bear left at a **Calderdale Way** sign, on a faint path uphill. Head for the wall at the top of the hill. Follow the wall to the left; then turn right, still following the wall, to walk on a

WHERE TO EAT AND DRINK ⓘ

Your best choice is the **Moorcock Inn**, close to where you parked. This is a popular meeting place for the local walking and rambling clubs – either before their walk on the moors or after.

path that becomes enclosed between walls as you leave the open moorland behind. At a fork of paths, keep straight ahead before going right, along a farm track to emerge at the **Spring Rock Restaurant**.

② Cross the road and continue on the narrowest of walled paths opposite the restaurant. Extensive views open up as the path goes right, down stone steps. Where the walled path ends, go left on a grassy path. Keep left of cottages on a good track. When you meet a fork of tracks, keep right, downhill, and immediately take a path that bears slightly to the left, into a small wood. The path soon descends to cross a stream on a stone-slab bridge, and bears right uphill to meet a walled track. Continue straight ahead on a path that passes a mill dam, then the mill itself, and on to a cobbled lane which emerges at a road, the B6113.

③ Walk right, along the road, for 150yds (138m) and take a good track on the left, **Moor Bottom Lane**. Continue along this ruler-

WHILE YOU'RE THERE ⓘ

After years of dereliction, the canal marina in **Sowerby Bridge** is slowly coming back to life. The centre of town was closed off to traffic for almost a year, while a filled-in section of canal was opened up to boats once again. This was made possible by building what is now – at 15ft (more than 5m) – the deepest canal lock in the country.

straight track, ignoring side-turnings, to enter **North Dean Wood** (from here you follow signs and arrows for the **Calderdale Way**). Keep left where the path forks to walk along the left-hand edge of the woodland, following a wall. Go uphill, over a stile, and on to a field path, still keeping the wood to your right. Join a track that soon meets a minor road. Go right, down to a sharp right-hand bend.

WHAT TO LOOK FOR ⓘ

The plateau of Norland Moor, overlooking Sowerby Bridge and the Calder Valley, is a particular delight in late summer, when the **heather** is in purple flower. Although we now consider heather to be the natural plant to grow on these moors, its introduction is relatively recent. Heather will not grow in the shade, and so it was not until all the trees had been cleared off these hills by early settlers that it really took a hold. You should also look for the bitter-sweet tasting bilberry, which is a favourite with grazing sheep around the end of June, and the less palatable (and mildly poisonous) crowberries, which cluster on rockier ground.

④ From here you bear left, following the **Calderdale Way** sign, on a stony track across **Norland Moor**. As you pass a pylon, take a path that keeps just to the right of the line of pylons ahead. You can soon take one of a choice of paths to the right, to reach the well-defined edge of **Norland Moor** once again, and back to your car.

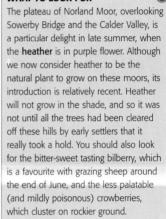

Bingley and the St Ives Estate

Great views of Airedale from a viewpoint known as the Druid's Altar.

•DISTANCE•	5½ miles (8.8km)
•MINIMUM TIME•	3hrs
•ASCENT / GRADIENT•	525ft (160m) ▲▲
•LEVEL OF DIFFICULTY•	🚶 🚶
•PATHS•	Good paths and tracks throughout, 2 stiles
•LANDSCAPE•	Woodland, park and river
•SUGGESTED MAP•	aqua3 OS Explorer 288 Bradford & Huddersfield
•START / FINISH•	Grid reference: SE 107393
•DOG FRIENDLINESS•	Can be off lead on St Ives Estate
•PARKING•	Car parks in Bingley
•PUBLIC TOILETS•	In Myrtle Park, Bingley

BACKGROUND TO THE WALK

Sitting astride both the River Aire and the Leeds and Liverpool Canal, in a steep-sided valley, Bingley is a typical West Yorkshire town. With its locks, wharfs and plethora of mills, the town grew in size and importance during the 19th century as the textile trades expanded. But Bingley's pre-eminence did not begin with the Industrial Revolution; it is, in fact, one of the county's oldest settlements, with its market charter being granted by King John as far back as 1212.

In keeping with its age, Bingley has a number of splendid old buildings, such as the town hall, parish church, butter cross, the old market hall and the Old White Horse, a venerable coaching inn. Ancient and modern sit side-by-side in Bingley, which has more than its fair share of architectural monstrosities, dating from more recent times. The headquarters of the Bradford & Bingley Building Society is perhaps a case in point.

Halliwell Sutcliffe, author of such books as *The Striding Dales* and *By Moor and Fell*, lived in Bingley while his father was headmaster of the town's Grammar School.

River Aire

The River Aire rises close to the village of Malham, in the limestone dales of North Yorkshire, and flows past Bingley. By the time it joins the Ouse and decants into the Humber Estuary it has been one of the hardest worked watercourses in Yorkshire. When the textile trades were at their height, the Aire was both a source of power for the woollen mills and a convenient dumping ground for industrial waste. But, like so many other West Yorkshire rivers, the water quality is now greatly improved.

St Ives

For part of this walk, you will be exploring the St Ives Estate which, from 1636, was owned by one of Bingley's most prominent families, the Ferrands. It was William Ferrand who, during the 1850s, landscaped the estate and created many of the paths and tracks that climb steeply up through the woods. The view from the top of the hill is ample reward for your efforts. From the gritstone outcrop known – somewhat fancifully – as the Druid's Altar, you have a splendid panorama across Bingley and the Aire Valley.

There is an inscription on Lady Blantyre's Rock, passed later on this walk, which commemorates William Ferrand's mother-in-law. Lady Blantyre often used to sit in the shade of this rock and read a book. A splendid notion: a monument to idleness. Near by is an obelisk with a dedication to William Ferrand himself. St Ives, a little wooded oasis on Bingley's doorstep, is now looked after by Bradford council on behalf of local people.

Walk 28 Directions

① Walk downhill from the centre of **Bingley**, towards the church. Go left at the traffic lights, passing the **Old White Horse** pub, on to **Millgate**. Cross the River Aire and take the first right, **Ireland Street**, veering right past industrial buildings to join a riverside track.

Very soon you seem to have swapped town for country. Bear right in front of **Ravenroyd Farm**, to pass between other farm buildings and continue on a walled track. Pass another house, **Cophurst**, and through pasture, with thick woodland on your left.

② The track skirts a hillock and approaches **Marley Farm**.

Walk 28

Go through a metal gate on the left, to continue on a field path that soon emerges on to a more substantial track. Bear left, immediately, by **Blakey Cottage**, on a setted (paved) track uphill. You soon gain height, passing two more farms, with views of **Airedale** opening up on the right. The track bears left and, after 100yds (91m), left again. At this point look for a stile ahead of you and take a narrow path that climbs steeply up through bracken. Keep left at a fork of tracks to the top of the hill to enjoy level walking with a wall on your right. Cross a track to arrive, just 100yds (91m) further on, at a rocky outcrop, known as the **Druid's Altar**, which offers splendid views.

> **WHAT TO LOOK FOR** ℹ
>
> Having been removed from the main street, Bingley's ancient stocks, butter cross and old market hall were re-sited near to the Ferrands Arms and the entrance to Myrtle Park.

③ Bear right, after the rocks, to come to a meeting of tracks. Go through a gap in the wall ahead, on to a walled track that leads into the **St Ives Estate**. Bear immediately to the right, through a gap stile in a wall, to take a path with woodland to your right and open fields to your left. After ½ mile (800m) you come to a kissing gate in the wall on your right, but your route is left here, into the woods and between golf fairways. At a choice of paths ahead, take the right-hand option, soon having a wall on your left and heather heathland on your right. Follow the path downhill, passing **Lady Blantyre's Rock**.

④ Ignoring side-tracks, follow the path downhill, past exuberant displays of rhododendrons, to

> **WHILE YOU'RE THERE** ℹ
>
> Next to Bingley is the little town of **Cottingley** where, in 1917, two young girls took photographs of fairies by Cottingley Beck. Despite the fairies looking like paper cut-outs, the pictures were 'authenticated' by Arthur Conan Doyle, creator of the fiercely logical Sherlock Holmes. Pay a visit to Cottingley Beck, and listen out for the beating of tiny wings...

Coppice Pond. Join a metalled road to bear left, soon passing a stable block, golf clubhouse and the house itself, **St Ives**.

⑤ Bear right past the house, to follow the house's drive downhill. Just 100yds (91m) before the road, take a path, left, through woodland. Keep right where the track forks, to reach the B6429, the Bingley to Cullingworth road. Cross it and continue downhill on narrow **Beckfoot Lane**. After houses the lane becomes an unmade track leading down to a delectable spot: here you will find **Beckfoot Farm**, in a wooded setting by **Harden Beck**, with a ford and an old packhorse bridge that dates back to 1723.

⑥ Cross the bridge and bear left at **Beckfoot Farm**, to find allotments on your left. Where the allotments end, take a path to the left which leads to a metal footbridge over the **River Aire** and into **Myrtle Park**. Cross the park to arrive once again in the centre of **Bingley**.

> **WHERE TO EAT AND DRINK** ℹ
>
> The oldest pub in Bingley is the 16th-century **Old White Horse Inn**, which you pass early on in this walk. It has oodles of character: that patina of age just can't be faked (no matter how hard the big pub chains try).

Bingley and the Five Rise Locks

Along the Leeds and Liverpool Canal from the centre of town to an elegant solution to a canal-building problem.
See map and information panel for Walk 28

•DISTANCE•	1½ miles (2.4km)
•MINIMUM TIME•	1hr
•ASCENT / GRADIENT•	98ft (30m) ▲▲ ▲▲ ▲▲
•LEVEL OF DIFFICULTY•	🚶🚶 🚶🚶 🚶🚶

Walk 29 Directions (Walk 28 option)

Walkers with an interest in canal history may want to extend Walk 28 to include a visit to Bingley's famous 'staircase' of locks which, after the Damart factory (makers of thermal underwear), is Bingley's best-known landmark. The Leeds and Liverpool Canal is, at 127 miles (205km), the longest canal in Britain. It was the first of the three trans-Pennine canals to be started, in 1770, and the last to be finished, in 1816. Unlike many of the other watercourses built during the years of 'canal mania', the Leeds and Liverpool proved to be profitable almost immediately.

The canal achieved its stated principal aim – giving easier access to overseas markets through the port of Liverpool for the mill owners of West Yorkshire. It cut the costs of transport in the heartlands of the textile industry, helping to bring considerable prosperity to towns like Bingley, Shipley and Keighley, that were largely dependent on the wool trade.

Access from the centre of town to the **Leeds and Liverpool Canal** is down **Park Road**. Cross the canal and take a path to the left that leads you to the tow path.

To cope with the undulating topography of the trans-Pennine route, there are 91 locks on the Leeds and Liverpool Canal, of which no fewer than eight can be found on this short stretch of the canal near Bingley. The three-rise locks are just a short walk of 300yds (274m) away, while the more celebrated five-rise locks are about ½ mile (800m) further on. In a remarkable feat of engineering, the rise of five locks lifts the level of the canal about 66ft (20m) in a space of just 100yds (91m). It can take some time for narrowboats to negotiate this picturesque bottleneck, but, after all, if people are in a hurry they will pick another mode of transport.

If you return via the tow path to the **Three Rise Locks**, you will find a cobbled ginnel on the right, known as **Treacle Cock Alley**, that takes you beneath the railway line and back into **Bingley** near the parish church.

Walk 30

By Canal and River from Rodley

A pleasant walk, along the banks of the River Aire and the Leeds and Liverpool Canal, that shows the rural face of Leeds.

•DISTANCE•	4 miles (6.4km)
•MINIMUM TIME•	2hrs
•ASCENT / GRADIENT•	33ft (10m) ▲ ▲ ▲
•LEVEL OF DIFFICULTY•	🚶 🚶 🚶
•PATHS•	Riverside path and canal tow path, 1 stile
•LANDSCAPE•	Surprisingly rural, considering you are so close to Leeds
•SUGGESTED MAP•	aqua3 OS Explorer 288 Bradford & Huddersfield
•START / FINISH•	Grid reference: SE 223364
•DOG FRIENDLINESS•	Can be off lead on most of walk
•PARKING•	Rodley, by Leeds and Liverpool Canal, close to swing bridge
•PUBLIC TOILETS•	None on route

Walk 30 Directions

The Leeds and Liverpool Canal starts at the canal basin in Leeds, where it links up with the Aire and Calder Navigation. From here it begins a journey of 127 miles (205km) across the Pennines. The canal was built between 1770 and 1816, with the Leeds–Skipton section being opened, to a fanfare, on 8 April, 1773. Two boatloads of coal arrived at Skipton Wharf that day, and were sold at half the normal price. That's an indication of just how important it was, for local industries, to create good transport links. Those towns through which the canal ran could look forward to a profitable future; those the canal avoided were likely to struggle.

For a few years the country was gripped by 'canal mania', and many waterways were built on a speculative basis. Only a few canals, including the Leeds and Liverpool, actually made money for their investors; many more proved to be expensive white elephants. And even the most successful canals were rendered obsolete with the coming of the railways. Though the Leeds and Liverpool Canal is no longer used for commercial traffic, it is navigable throughout its length. Canal craft today are recreational, with boating enthusiasts being able to take a leisurely route from the heart of Leeds up to Skipton and Gargrave, on the fringes of the Yorkshire Dales.

WHAT TO LOOK FOR ⓘ

The canal here, and as far as Armley towards Leeds and Apperley Bridge towards Shipley, has been designated a Site of Special Scientific Interest (SSSI) because of the range of aquatic life it supports. On the surface this includes coots, moorhens, ducks and swans, whilst below the waterline you may spot a pike lurking in the depths. Look out, too, for kingfishers and wagtails.

Walk 30

Cross the canal on the swing bridge, and bear left along the broad tow path to pass beneath the bridge that carries the ring road. Walk for another 150yds (138m), and turn right after another canal swing bridge, on a paved lane between houses. Go left, almost immediately, to follow a path down steps and across the **River Aire** on an old stone bridge.

Bear right, on the far side of the river, through a gap stile, to join a riverside path. Walk under the ring road again, and continue on the path, signed as 'Riverside Path to Newlaithes Road'. When the river bends to the right, your path goes left, uphill, through a metal kissing gate. Keep straight ahead on a field path, parallel to a railway line on the left, and following a wall. Take a kissing gate, and follow a path between fences, to cross the railway line on a footbridge. You emerge into a housing estate, where you turn right, along **Newlaithes Road**. 100yds (91m) before a T-junction, take steps to the right and continue down a road, **Newlay Lane**, to a metal bridge over the **River Aire**.

Cross the river and continue up the road, passing the **Abbey Inn**. Go left, just before a bridge, to gain access to the tow path of the **Leeds and Liverpool Canal**. Go right, under the bridge, soon passing a boatyard and a swing bridge near a mill. By some industrial units is another swing bridge (and an access road to **Rodley Nature Reserve**, whose wildfowl-rich meres are accessible at weekends). Continue along the canal tow path to arrive back in **Rodley**.

Standedge from Marsden

A classic moorland ramble on the ancient Rapes Highway.

•DISTANCE•	6½ miles (10.4km)
•MINIMUM TIME•	3hrs 30min
•ASCENT / GRADIENT•	900ft (375m) ▲▲ ▲▲
•LEVEL OF DIFFICULTY•	👫 👫 👫
•PATHS•	Old tracks and byways, canal tow path, 5 stiles
•LANDSCAPE•	Heather moorland
•SUGGESTED MAP•	aqua3 OS Outdoor Leisure 21 South Pennines
•START / FINISH•	Grid reference: SE 048117
•DOG FRIENDLINESS•	Keep under control where sheep graze on open moorland
•PARKING•	Free street parking in Marsden
•PUBLIC TOILETS•	Marsden, at start of walk

BACKGROUND TO THE WALK

Trans-Pennine travel has, until quite recently, been a hazardous business. Over the centuries many routes have been driven across the hills to link the industrial centres of West Yorkshire and Lancashire. Some paths were consolidated into paved causeways for packhorse traffic, before being upgraded to take vehicles. This track, linking the Colne Valley to the Lancashire towns of Rochdale and Milnrow, was known as the Rapes Highway.

The Standedge Tunnel

This was tough terrain for building a canal. When the Huddersfield Narrow Canal was cut, to provide a link between Huddersfield and Ashton-under-Lyne, there was one major obstacle for the canal builders to overcome. The gritstone bulk of Standedge straddled the county border. There was no way round; the canal had to go through. The Standedge Tunnel, extending 3 miles (4.8km) from Marsden to Diggle, was a monumental feat of engineering. Costly in every sense, it took 16 years to build and many navvies lost their lives. The result was the longest, highest and deepest canal tunnel in the country.

In an attempt to keep those costs down, the tunnel was cut as narrow as possible, which left no room for a tow path. Towing horses had to be led over the hills to the far end of the tunnel, near the little Lancashire town of Diggle. The bargees had to negotiate Standedge Tunnel using their own muscle power alone. This method, known as 'legging', required the boatmen to lie on their backs and push with their feet against the sides and roof of the tunnel. This operation would typically take a back-breaking 4 hours; it would have been a great relief to see the proverbial light at the end of the tunnel. Closed to canal traffic for many years, the tunnel is currently being restored for recreational users (at least those with strong legs and backs).

In 1812 Marsden became the focus for the 'Luddite' rebellion against mechanisation in the textile industry. A secret group of croppers and weavers banded together to break up the new machinery which was appearing in local mills and which had been developed by local industrialists. The rebellion caused much consternation and eventually the army was despatched to restore order. Sixty men were put on trial in York for their part in the troubles; 17 of them were subsequently hanged.

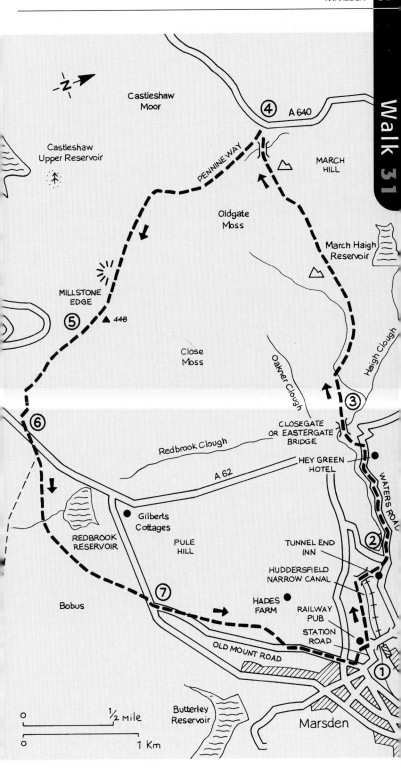

Walk 31

Walk 31 Directions

① From the centre of **Marsden**, take **Station Road**, uphill. Between the **Railway** pub, and the station itself, go left along the tow path of the **Huddersfield Narrow Canal**. At **Tunnel End** – where both canal and train lines disappear into a tunnel through the hillside – cross the canal on a footbridge, and walk up a track to the **Tunnel End Inn**.

WHAT TO LOOK FOR ⓘ

In spring and early summer, listen out for a **cuckoo**. If an old story is to be believed, the people of Marsden realised that when the **cuckoo** arrived, so did the sunshine. They tried to keep spring forever, by building a tower around the cuckoo. As the last stones were about to be laid, however, the cuckoo flew away. The good folk of Marsden use the joke against themselves, and now celebrate Cuckoo Day in April each year.

---

② Walk left along **Waters Road**. Keep straight ahead after ½ mile (800m), at the entrance to the **Hey Green Hotel.**100yds (91m) further on, bear left, just before a cottage, on to a footpath. The path takes you across **Closegate Bridge**, known locally as **Eastergate Bridge**, where two becks meet.

③ Keep right, following the right-hand beck for about 100yds (91m), when the path bears left, up a steep side-valley. The path levels off at the top and then bears slightly right, towards the rounded prominence of **March Hill**. Your route across moorland is soon marked by a series of waymarker stones, though your way ahead is unmistakable. After a few ups and downs, the path rises steeply uphill, before descending towards the A640.

④ Just before you reach the road, take a wooden bridge over a little beck and follow a **Pennine Way** sign on a track that bears acute left. Take this well-maintained gravel track uphill. After a few minutes you follow the contours of **Millstone Edge,** a rocky ridge that offers panoramic views into **East Lancashire**. Just before the trig point is a plaque commemorating Amon Wrigley, a local poet.

⑤ Your route is downhill from here. Take a succession of stiles in walls and fences before going left on an unmade track that leads down to the A62, where a car park overlooks **Brunclough Reservoir**.

⑥ Cross the road and take steps up to the left of the car park, signed 'Pennine Way', to access a good track, soon revealing views to the left of **Redbrook Reservoir** and **Pule Hill** beyond. At a marker stone the **Pennine Way** bears right. But your route – having made a small detour to cross a tiny beck – is to continue along the track. It gradually sweeps left, around the slopes of **Pule Hill**, to reach a road.

WHERE TO EAT AND DRINK ⓘ

Marsden is not short of characterful pubs, but the two most convenient watering holes on this walk are the **Railway** and the **Tunnel End Inn** (near the railway station and Tunnel End, respectively and predictably).

---

⑦ Turn right, along the road, but then immediately left, up **Old Mount Road**. After 100yds (91m), bear left again, up a stony track signed to **Hades** farm. After ½ mile (800m), take a path to the right, that accompanies a wall, to rejoin **Old Mount Road**. Follow the road downhill to arrive back in **Marsden**.

Haworth's Brontë Moors

Across the wild Pennine moors to the romantic ruin of Top Withins.

•**DISTANCE**•	7½ miles (12km)
•**MINIMUM TIME**•	3hrs 30min
•**ASCENT / GRADIENT**•	650ft (200m) ▲▲▲
•**LEVEL OF DIFFICULTY**•	쏏쏏 쏏쏏 쏏쏏
•**PATHS**•	Well-signed and easy to follow, 2 stiles
•**LANDSCAPE**•	Open Moorland
•**SUGGESTED MAP**•	aqua3 OS Outdoor Leisure 21 South Pennines
•**START / FINISH**•	Grid reference: SE 029373
•**DOG FRIENDLINESS**•	Under control near sheep on open moorland
•**PARKING**•	Pay-and-display car park, near Brontë Parsonage
•**PUBLIC TOILETS**•	Central Park, Haworth

BACKGROUND TO THE WALK

Who could have imagined, when the Revd Patrick Brontë became curate of the Church of St Michael and All Angels in 1820, that the little gritstone town of Haworth would become a literary Mecca to rival Grasmere and Stratford-upon-Avon? But it has, and visitors flock here in great numbers: some to gain some insights into the works of Charlotte, Emily and Anne, others just to enjoy a day out.

If the shy sisters could see the Haworth of today, they would recognise the steep, cobbled main street. But they would no doubt be amazed to see the tourist industry that's built up to exploit their names and literary reputations. They would recognise the Georgian parsonage too. Now a museum, it has been painstakingly restored to reflect the lives of the Brontës and the rooms are filled with their personal treasures.

That three such prodigious talents should be found within a single family is remarkable enough. To have created such towering works as *Jane Eyre* and *Wuthering Heights* while living in what was a bleakly inhospitable place is almost beyond belief. The public were unprepared for this trio of lady novelists, which is why all the books published during their lifetimes bore the androgynous pen-names of Currer, Ellis and Acton Bell.

From the day that Patrick Brontë came to Haworth with his wife and six children, tragedy was never far away. His wife died the following year and two daughters did not live to adulthood. His only son Branwell succumbed to drink and drugs; Anne and Emily died aged 29 and 30 respectively. Charlotte, alone, lived long enough to marry. But after just one year of marriage – to her father's curate – she too fell ill and died in 1855, at the age of 38. Revd Brontë survived them all, living to the ripe old age of 84.

Tourism is no recent development; by the middle of the 19th century the first literary pilgrims were finding their way to Haworth. No matter how crowded this little town becomes (and those who value their solitude should avoid visiting on a sunny summer weekend) it is always possible to escape to the moors that surround the town. You can follow, literally, in the footsteps of the three sisters as they sought freedom and inspiration, away from the stifling confines of the parsonage and the adjacent graveyard. As you explore these inhospitable moors, you'll get a greater insight into the literary world of the Brontës than those who stray no further than the souvenir shops and tea rooms of Haworth.

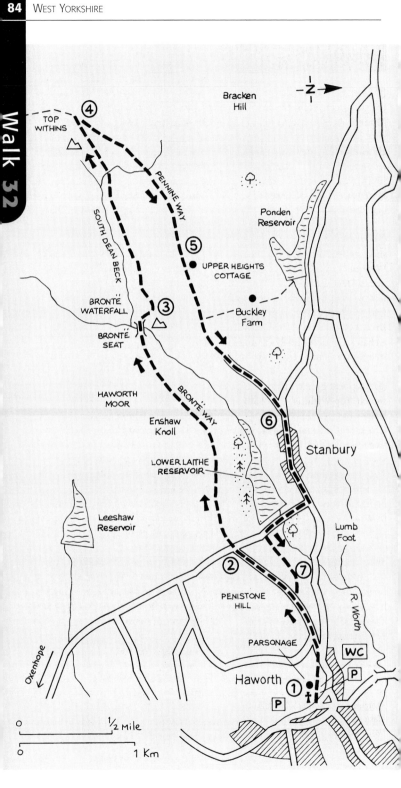

Walk 32 Directions

① Take the cobbled lane up past the parsonage, signed to **Haworth Moor**. The lane soon becomes a paved field path that leads to the **Haworth–Stanbury** road. Walk left along the road and, after just 75yds (68m), take a left fork, signed to **Penistone Hill**. Continue along this quiet road to a T-junction.

② Take the track straight ahead, soon signed '**Brontë Way** and **Top Withins**', gradually descending to **South Dean Beck** where, within a few paces of the stone bridge, you'll find the **Brontë Waterfall** and **Brontë Seat** (a stone that resembles a chair). Cross the bridge and climb steeply uphill to a three-way sign.

③ Keep left, uphill, on a paved path signed '**Top Withins**'. The path levels out to accompany a wall. Cross a beck on stepping stones; a steep uphill climb brings you to a waymarker by a ruined building. Take a short detour of 200yds (183m), left, uphill, to visit the ruin of **Top Withins,** possibly the inspiration for Wuthering Heights.

④ Turn right at the waymarker, on a paved path, downhill, signed to **Stanbury** and **Haworth**; you are now joining the **Pennine Way**. You have a broad, easily-followed track across the wide expanse of wild Pennine moorland.

⑤ Pass a white farmhouse – **Upper Heights Cottage** – then bear immediately left at a fork of tracks (still signed here as the **Pennine Way**). Walk past another building, **Lower Heights Farm**. After 500yds (456m) you come to another fork: where the **Pennine Way** veers off to the left, you should continue on the track straight ahead, signed to **Stanbury** and **Haworth**. Follow the track to meet a road near the village of **Stanbury**.

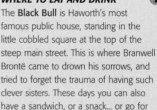

WHERE TO EAT AND DRINK ⓘ

The **Black Bull** is Haworth's most famous public house, standing in the little cobbled square at the top of the steep main street. This is where Branwell Brontë came to drown his sorrows, and tried to forget the trauma of having such clever sisters. These days you can also have a sandwich, or a snack... or go for the Full Brontë.

⑥ Bear right along the road through **Stanbury**, then take the first road on the right, signed to **Oxenhope**, and cross the dam of **Lower Laithe Reservoir**. Immediately beyond the dam, bear left on a road that is soon reduced to a track uphill, to meet a road by **Haworth Cemetery**.

⑦ From here you retrace your outward route: walk left along the road, soon taking a gap stile on the right, to follow the paved field path back into **Haworth**.

WHILE YOU'RE THERE ⓘ

At the bottom of that famous cobbled street is Haworth Station, on the restored **Keighley and Worth Valley Railway**. Take a steam train journey on Britain's last remaining complete branch line railway. Or browse through the books and railway souvenirs at the station shop.

WHAT TO LOOK FOR ⓘ

The Brontës are 'big in Japan'. It seems that the Japanese have an almost insatiable appetite to learn about the sisters' lives and books. So don't be surprised to find that a lot of signs in the town – and on the walk to Top Withins too – are written in English and Japanese. Strange but true.

Walk 33

Ilkley Moor and the Twelve Apostles

Standing stones and a brief look at some of the intriguing historic features which make up Ilkley Moor.

•DISTANCE•	4½ miles (7.2km)
•MINIMUM TIME•	2hrs 30min
•ASCENT / GRADIENT•	425ft (130m) ▲▲▲
•LEVEL OF DIFFICULTY•	🚶🚶 🚶
•PATHS•	Good moorland paths, some steep paths towards end of walk, 4 stiles on Walk 34
•LANDSCAPE•	Mostly open heather moorland, and gritstone crags
•SUGGESTED MAP•	aqua3 OS Explorer 297 Lower Wharfedale
•START / FINISH•	Grid reference: SE 132467
•DOG FRIENDLINESS•	Under contol where sheep graze freely on moorland
•PARKING•	Off-road parking on Hangingstone Road, opposite Cow and Calf rocks, also a pay-and-display car park
•PUBLIC TOILETS•	In pay-and-display car park near Cow and Calf rocks

BACKGROUND TO THE WALK

Ilkley Moor is a long ridge of millstone grit, immediately to the south of Ilkley. With or without a hat, Ilkley Moor is a special place... not just for walkers, but for lovers of archaeological relics too. These extensive heather moors are identified on maps as Rombalds Moor, named after a legendary giant who roamed the area. But, thanks to the famous song – Yorkshire's unofficial anthem – Ilkley Moor is how it's always known.

An Ancient Ring

The Twelve Apostles is a ring of Bronze Age standing stones sited close to the meeting of two ancient routes across the moor. If you expect to find something of Stonehenge proportions, you will be disappointed. The twelve slabs of millstone grit (there were more stones originally, probably twenty, with one at the centre) are arranged in a circle approximately 50ft (15m) in diameter. The tallest of the stones is little more than 3ft (1m). The circle is, nevertheless, a genuinely ancient monument.

The Twelve Apostles are merely the most visible evidence of 7,000 years of occupation of these moors. There are other, smaller circles too, and Ilkley Moor is celebrated for its Bronze Age rock carvings, many showing the familiar 'cup and ring' designs. The most famous of these rocks features a sinuous swastika: traditionally a symbol of good luck, until the Nazis corrupted it. There are milestones, dating from more recent times, which would have given comfort and guidance to travellers across these lonely moors. In addition to Pancake and Haystack rocks, seen on this walk, there are dozens of other natural gritstone rock formations. The biggest and best known are the Cow and Calf, close to the start of this walk, where climbers practise their holds and rope work.

A guidebook of 1829 described Ilkley as a little village. It was the discovery of mineral springs that transformed Ilkley into a prosperous spa town. Dr William Mcleod arrived here

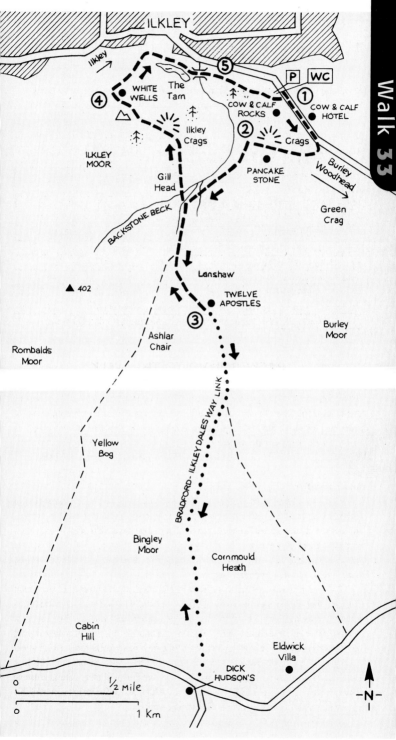

in 1847, recognised the town's potential and spent the next 25 years creating a place where well-heeled hypochondriacs could 'take the waters' in upmarket surroundings.

Dr Mcleod recognised – or perhaps just imagined – the curative properties of cold water. He vigorously promoted what he called the 'Ilkley Cure', a strict regime of exercise and cold baths. Luxurious hotels known as 'hydros', precursors of today's health farms, sprang up around the town to cater for the influx of visitors.

Predating the town's popularity as a spa is White Wells, built in 1700 around one of the original springs. A century later a pair of plunge baths were added, where visitors and locals alike could enjoy the masochistic pleasures of bathing in cold water. Enjoying extensive views over the town, the building is still painted white. White Wells is now a visitor centre that's open to (non-bathing) visitors at weekends.

Walk 33 Directions

① Walk up the road; 150yds (138m) beyond the **Cow and Calf Hotel**, where the road bears left, fork right up a grassy path. Scramble up the ridge to the **Pancake Stone**, and enjoy the extensive views back over **Ilkley** and **Wharfedale**. Bear right on a path along the edge of the ridge, cross a stony track and pass the **Haystack Rock**. From here your track slowly wheels left, to run parallel to **Backstone Beck**, uphill, on to open heather moorland.

② At the top you meet the **Bradford–Ilkley Dales Way** link path. Go left here; soon you are walking on a section of duckboarding. Pass a boundary stone at the top of the next rise, and continue to the ring of stones known as the **Twelve Apostles**.

③ Retrace your steps from the **Twelve Apostles**, and continue along the **Dales Way** link path. Having crossed **Backstone Beck**, you soon leave the open moorland behind, and find yourself on top of a ridge. Enjoy the views across **Ilkley** and **Wharfedale**, before taking the path (which is stepped in some in places) steeply downhill. Beneath a clump of trees you come to **White Wells**.

④ Bear right, passing to the left of ponds, on a path, downhill. Aim for a pyramid-shaped rock, after which you emerge on to a metalled track. Walk either way around the tarn. At the far end take a path, uphill at first, then down to cross **Backstone Beck** again on a little footbridge, then one last haul uphill to reach the **Cow and Calf** rocks.

⑤ It's worth taking a few minutes to investigate the rocks and watch climbers practising their belays and traverses. From here a paved path leads back to the car park.

WHILE YOU'RE THERE

Ilkley Moor is an intriguingly ancient landscape, criss-crossed by old tracks. These two walks offer a short and a long option, but you could explore for weeks without walking the same path twice. An east–west walk from the Cow and Calf will take you along the moorland ridge, with terrific views of Ilkley and Wharfedale for most of the way.

WHAT TO LOOK FOR

Many rocks on Ilkley Moor are decorated with 'cup and ring' patterns – including the **Pancake Rock**, near the start of this walk. Many more rock carvings can be found if you take the time to search for them.

Walk 34

Across Ilkley Moor to Dick Hudson's

A classic moorland ramble on an ancient path that's been walked since the Bronze Age.

See map and information panel for Walk 33

•DISTANCE•	8 miles (12.9km)
•MINIMUM TIME•	4hrs
•ASCENT / GRADIENT•	425ft (130m) ▲▲ ▲
•LEVEL OF DIFFICULTY•	👣 👣 👣

Walk 34 Directions (Walk 33 option)

Walk 34 is an extension of Walk 33, continuing beyond the Twelve Apostles stone circle, across Ilkley Moor, to the pub at Dick Hudson's. It's a classic walk enjoyed by many generations of ramblers. You can stride out across heather moorland, knowing that no matter what time of the day you arrive (within reason), you should be able to get a meal. Food is served each day from 12 noon to 9PM. Dick Hudson, incidentally, was a popular landlord of Queen Victoria's day; the pub's original name was the Fleece Inn.

Continue past the **Twelve Apostles** on a good moorland path, passing two more milestones; in places you are walking on causeway stones. This gently sloping upland heath is now the Bingley Moor section of the larger Rombalds Moor, and is dotted with evocative place names reflecting continuous use since ancient times. Eventually you make a slow descent to a gate in a wall, follow a fence and take a walled path that delivers you to

Dick Hudson's. A glance at the Ordnance Survey map will reveal a variety of return routes to **Ilkley**, though they all require some road-walking. The best route is to go back the same way you came, retracing your steps to the **Twelve Apostles**, then rejoining the route of Walk 33 from Point ③. Before you leave the summit ridge of the moor you may like to pick your way through the heather to the summit cairn, up to your left as you head towards Ilkley. On a clear day you'll be rewarded with far-reaching views which take in York Minster, Roseberry Topping and the White Horse at Kildburn.

> ### WHERE TO EAT AND DRINK ⓘ
> This classic walk across Ilkley Moor almost demands that you follow in the footsteps of generations of walkers, by calling in at **Dick Hudson's** for a hearty meal. The **Cow and Calf Hotel**, at the start of the walk, near the famous rocks, is another option for refreshments. If you've time to wander around Ilkley itself, the first hostelry you'll come to is the **Midland Hotel**, serving bar meals and real ales. Further along the street, on The Grove, you'll find a branch of the famous **Betty's Tea Rooms**, where dignified Ilkley ladies mingle with the tourists over tinkling piano music and speciality teas.

Fells of the Holme Valley

A short walk of great variety, from the unspoiled hill village of Hepworth.

•DISTANCE•	3 miles (4.8km)
•MINIMUM TIME•	1hr 30min
•ASCENT / GRADIENT•	525ft (160m) ▲▲▲
•LEVEL OF DIFFICULTY•	🚶 🚶 🚶
•PATHS•	Good tracks most of the way, 9 stiles
•LANDSCAPE•	Rolling countryside
•SUGGESTED MAP•	aqua3 OS Explorer 288 Bradford & Huddersfield
•START / FINISH•	Grid reference: SE 163068
•DOG FRIENDLINESS•	Plenty of opportunities to be off lead
•PARKING•	Hepworth, just off A616, south of Huddersfield
•PUBLIC TOILETS•	None on route

Walk 35 **Directions**

This short walk visits no stately home or famous landmark. It just takes in some delightful countryside which, in places, recalls the lower fells of Lakeland. To the south of Holmfirth, famous for its role in *Last of the Summer Wine,* are a number of villages whose fortunes rose with the cottage industry of hand weaving, then declined when weaving started to be organised on a truly industrial scale. Honley, Scholes, Jackson Bridge and Hepworth retain many of their old weavers' cottages, built of Yorkshire sandstone and millstone grit. The hilltop village of Hepworth, with no convenient source of water, never became industrialised.

Weavers' houses tend to conform to a traditional design: two or three stories high, with the weaving room occupying the whole length of the attic. Rows of narrow, mullioned windows allowed the maximum amount of light into the room. The weaving room was often reached by outside stairs and a 'taking in' door. This made it easier to bring woollen yarn in and take the finished pieces of cloth out. It also allowed a weaver to divide his life more conveniently between his work and his family responsibilities.

Another tradition, during the 16th and 17th centuries, was the 'dual economy' of textiles and farming. The land was poor, and generally unsuitable for growing crops, so the smallholders would keep dairy cows or sheep. Many weavers would have worked with wool spun from the fleeces of their own sheep. Substantial farmsteads – known as laithe-houses – combined, under one roof, family accommodation, a

---

WHAT TO LOOK FOR

The little stone village of **Hepworth** is surrounded by some of the finest countryside in the county; quiet lanes, stone walls and a wide choice of old paths to walk. The proximity of town and country is a striking feature of the area. One minute you are walking on tarmac and cobbles, but within a very few minutes you can be out on the tops.

Walk 35

WHERE TO EAT AND DRINK

The **Butchers Arms**, a real locals' pub in the middle of Hepworth village, is the place for a drink and – at weekends – good food. The **White Horse Inn** at Jackson Bridge – just north of Hepworth, off the A616 – may be familiar even to first-time visitors, since it has featured in many episodes of *Last of the Summer Wine*. Pictures taken from the comedy series are displayed inside.

hay barn for cattle and a weaving room beneath the eaves. Examples of these characterful buildings can still be seen in Hepworth and elsewhere in the Holme Valley.

From the **Butchers Arms**, walk through the village for 100yds (91m). Take steps on the left, immediately before the end-wall of a house; a field path takes you down into the valley. Follow a wall on your right and, towards the bottom of the hill, cross the wall by a stile. Continue walking downhill in the same direction, and cross a footbridge. Bear left on a path for just 100yds (91m) before going right, up stone steps. Follow the path uphill, over a stile, through trees, to meet a road.

Cross the road and take a metalled track ahead, between walls. Beyond a small lake on your left you have a choice of routes. Bear right, on a metalled track, steeply uphill. When the track goes left, to **Bank House Farm**, continue ahead on a stony path, which soon bears right. When the path bears sharp left, take a gate on your right. You now have easy walking on a grassy path, with extensive views across the valley. Through another gate, your route is joined by another track. Just before a farmhouse, look for a fingerpost on the right to take an indistinct

field path downhill. Beyond a gate your path is clearer, through trees and down to meet a road. Walk left along the road for just 75yds (68m) before taking a kissing gate on the right, by a driveway to a house. Cross the field to another gate then follow a fence downhill to a gap stile. Go left on a field path, following a wall, towards buildings ahead. Come to a wall stile at **Barnside** and go left to meet a road.

Go right down **Barnside Lane**. Take a footpath just past the house on the left, cross a stile and walk uphill, crossing two fields to meet a ladder stile at the top of the second field. Bear half right here, on a sketchy path; soon you have a ruined farmhouse to aim for.

Behind **Ox Lea Farm**, take a track to the right. Follow this hollow way (or the adjacent, drier path). Beyond a gate the walking is easier on a broad, walled track. At a crossroads, go straight ahead down **Cowcliff Hill Road**. After just 50yds (46m) take a wall stile on the right, between two metal gates. Follow this field path, keeping a wall to your right. After the next wall stile your path is across the middle of three fields, before joining a path between a wall and a fence. Soon you are back in **Hepworth**, as the path emerges at the side of the **Butchers Arms**.

WHILE YOU'RE THERE

Nearby **Jackson Bridge** is a cramped little community, wedged into a valley around the White Horse Inn. Here you will find rows of distinctive weavers' cottages. To save space, some houses are built on top of each other, providing 'underdwellings' and 'overdwellings', a building solution more familiar in places like Hebden Bridge.

Oxenhope and the Worth Valley Railway

A moorland round and a return to the age of steam.

•DISTANCE•	6 miles (9.7km)
•MINIMUM TIME•	3hrs
•ASCENT / GRADIENT•	492ft (150m) ▲▲ ▲▲ ▲
•LEVEL OF DIFFICULTY•	🚶🚶 🚶🚶 🚶
•PATHS•	Good paths and tracks, 6 stiles
•LANDSCAPE•	Upland scenery, moor and pasture
•SUGGESTED MAP•	aqua3 OS Outdoor Leisure 21 South Pennines
•START / FINISH•	Grid reference: SE 033354
•DOG FRIENDLINESS•	Keep on lead along country lanes
•PARKING•	Street parking in Oxenhope, near Keighley and Worth Valley Railway station
•PUBLIC TOILETS•	None on route

BACKGROUND TO THE WALK

Oxenhope is at the end of the line in more ways than one. As well as being the terminus of the Keighley and Worth Valley Railway, Oxenhope is the last village in the Worth Valley. To the north are Haworth and Keighley; going south, into Calderdale and Hebden Bridge, requires you to gear down for a scenic drive over the lonely heights of Cock Hill.

Oxenhope was a farming community that expanded, like many other villages in West Yorkshire, with the textile industry. The mills, however, have mostly disappeared, leaving the village to commuters who work in nearby towns. Apart from the railway, the village is best known for the Oxenhope Straw Race, held each year on the first Sunday in July. Competitors have to carry a bale of straw around the village, while drinking as much beer as possible. Whoever finishes this assault course first, it is the local charities that benefit most.

Keighley and Worth Valley Railway

The Keighley and Worth Valley line, running for 5 miles (8km) from Keighley to Oxenhope, is one of the longest established private railways in the country, and the last remaining complete branch line. It was built in 1867, funded by local mill owners, but the trains were run by the Midland Railway to link to the main Leeds–Skipton line at Keighley.

When the line fell victim to Dr Beeching's axe in 1962, local rail enthusiasts banded together in opposition to the closure. The preservation society bought the line: a pioneering example of rail privatisation. Thus began a major restoration of the line and the stations. Ingrow station, for example, had been so badly vandalised that a complete station was 'transported' to the site stone by stone from Foulridge in Lancashire. Built to the typical Midland style, it now blends in well with the other stations on the line.

By 1968 the society began running a regular timetable of trains that has continued ever since. Steam trains run every weekend throughout the year, and daily in summer. But the line doesn't just cater for tourists; locals in the Worth Valley appreciate the diesel services into Keighley which operate on almost 200 days per year.

Walk 36

The line runs through the heart of Brontë country, with stations at Oxenhope, Haworth, Oakworth, Danems, Ingrow and Keighley. The stations are a particular delight: fully restored, gas-lit and redolent of the age of steam. So when Edith Nesbitt's classic children's novel, *The Railway Children*, was being filmed in 1970, the Keighley and Worth Valley Railway was a natural choice of setting. And Oakworth station – a splendid example of an Edwardian station, complete with enamel advertising signs – is the one used in the film. Everyone who has seen the film (it's the one with Jenny Agutter in and it seems to be etched deeply into the national psyche) will enjoy revisiting the much-loved locations.

Walk 36

Walk 36 **Directions**

① From the entrance of **Oxenhope Station** take the minor road to the left, up to the A6033. Cross the road and take **Dark Lane** ahead, a sunken lane that goes steeply uphill. Follow this track to a road. Go right here, downhill, to join the **Denholme road** (B6141). Walk left along the road, up to the **Dog and Gun** pub, where you turn right on to **Sawood Lane**.

WHERE TO EAT AND DRINK ⓘ

At about the half-way point, this walk passes the **Waggon & Horses**, an isolated pub on the Hebden Bridge Road out of Oxenhope. The pub enjoys great views over the valley towards Haworth and the moors, and has a good reputation for its food. If you decide to take the train there's an excellent café at **Oxenhope Station**, appropriately enough in a stationary British Rail buffet car.

---

② At **Coblin Farm**, your route becomes a rough track. Go through a gate to join a metalled road to the right, uphill, signed **Brontë Way**. After 100yds (91m), when the road accesses **Thornton Moor Reservoir**, walk straight ahead on an unmade track. Go through a gate into rough pasture, ignoring the **Brontë Way** sign to the right.

③ At a fork, just 50yds (46m) further on, keep right as the track goes downhill towards a transmission mast on the mid-horizon. Pass a clump of trees, and cross a watercourse before descending to a minor road.

④ Go right here to pass a cattle grid and the mast. 150yds (138m) beyond the mast, as the road begins a steep descent, take a wall stile on

the left. Go through another wall stile, to walk left, uphill, on a broad, walled track that deposits you at the **Waggon and Horses** pub.

⑤ Cross the road and take a track between gateposts, which bears right, steeply downhill. Where it bears sharp right again, after 300yds (274m), take a stile to the left, by a gate. Follow a wall downhill to take three stiles in succession; at the bottom you meet a walled path. Go left here, cross a stream, and continue uphill to arrive at the entrance to **Lower Fold Farm**.

⑥ Follow the farm track to the right; turn right again, 20yds (18m) further on, at the end of a cottage, to join a metalled track. The track soon bears right above **Leeshaw Reservoir** and makes a gradual descent. Pass a mill to meet a road.

WHAT TO LOOK FOR

Visiting **Oxenhope Station** is like going back a hundred years. It has been lovingly restored, with enough period detail to make steam buffs dewy-eyed with nostalgia.

---

⑦ Cross the road and take the track ahead (signed to **Marsh**). Keep right of the first house, on a narrow walled path, then a paved path. Pass through the courtyard of a house as the path goes left, then right, and through a kissing gate. Follow a path between a wall and a fence to meet a walled lane. Go right here, passing houses, then on a field path to meet a road. Go right here and back down into **Oxenhope**.

WHILE YOU'RE THERE ⓘ

Take a trip to Haworth and back on the **Keighley and Worth Valley Railway**, and relive the great days of steam. You can return on foot along the Worth Way.

Laycock and Goose Eye

A varied walk, from intimate woodlands to the breezy moor-tops.

•DISTANCE•	8 miles (12.9km)
•MINIMUM TIME•	4hrs
•ASCENT / GRADIENT•	656ft (200m) ▲▲▲
•LEVEL OF DIFFICULTY•	🚶🚶 🚶🚶 🚶🚶
•PATHS•	Good paths and tracks, take care with route finding, 8 stiles
•LANDSCAPE•	Wooded valley and heather moorland
•SUGGESTED MAP•	aqua3 OS Outdoor Leisure 21 South Pennines
•START / FINISH•	Grid reference: SE 035412
•DOG FRIENDLINESS•	Under control where sheep graze on sections of moorland
•PARKING•	In Laycock village, roadside parking at Keighley end of village, close to village hall
•PUBLIC TOILETS•	None on route

BACKGROUND TO THE WALK

To the west of Keighley a tranche of moorland sits astride the border between Yorkshire and Lancashire. Here you can walk for miles without seeing another hiker – and perhaps with just curlew and grouse for company. When we think of textile mills, we tend to associate them with cramped towns full of smoking chimneys. But the earliest mills were sited in surprisingly rural locations, often in the little steep-sided valleys known as cloughs where fast-flowing becks and rivers could be dammed and diverted to turn the waterwheels. There are reminders, in wooded Newsholme Dean, that even a watercourse as small as Dean Beck could be harnessed to provide power to a cotton mill in Goose Eye. Weirs along the beck helped to maintain a good head of water, and one of the mill dams is now popular with anglers.

Laycock and Goose Eye

The village of Laycock contains a number of handsome old houses in the typical South Pennine style. While Laycock sits on the hillside, with good valley views, neighbouring Goose Eye nestles in a hollow. The village was originally called 'Goose Heights', which the local dialect contracted to 'Goose Ay', and thence to the name we know today. Lovers of real ale will already be familiar with the name, as this is the home of the Goose Eye Brewery.

Walk 37 Directions

① Walk through the village of **Laycock**. Where the road narrows, go left down a paved track, **Roberts Street**. Pass terraced houses to join a narrow walled path. You emerge on to a road, which you follow down into **Goose Eye**. Pass the **Turkey Inn**, the only pub on this walk. Just 50yds (46m) after you cross **Dean Beck**, take the steps on your right and re-cross the beck on a footbridge. Follow the beck upstream and take a footbridge on the right, across a water channel (now empty).

Walk **37**

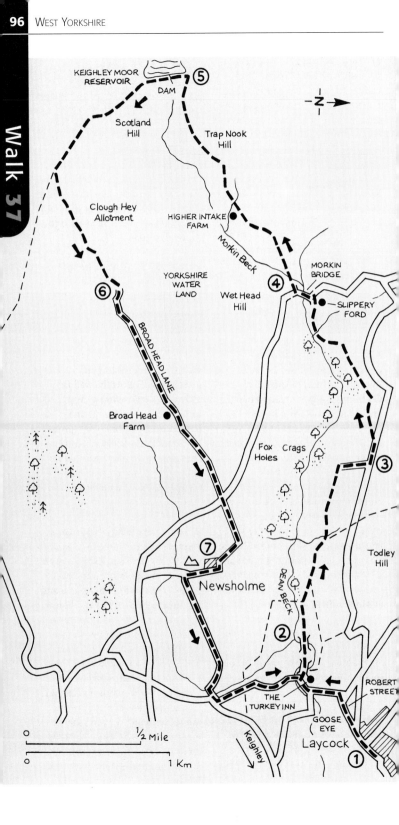

Walk 37

② Pass a mill dam, soon enjoying easy walking, above the beck. Bear right up a paved path, levelling out between pasture and scrubland. Pass the rear of a farmhouse, and cross a stony track, to continue in the same direction, via a gate, along a track (signed to **Slippery Ford**). Continue uphill, through another gate and across a stream to a choice of tracks. Keep right, up a hollow way (or the adjacent path). Your path, soon paved, goes through a gate and up to meet a road.

③ Walk left, along the road, for 75yds (68m), before taking the access track on the left down to **Bottoms Farm**. Keep right of farm buildings to take a gate on the right. A path comes to a stile at the far end of a barn. Follow the path towards the head of the valley. Go through a gate to take a path, and stiles, across three fields in front of a farmhouse. At the bottom of the third field, you reach a point where two becks meet to form **Dean Beck**. Cross the beck in front of you, go through a gate and follow the other beck to a wall. Accompany the wall to the right, uphill, and take a gate on the left into the yard of **Slitheroford Farm**. Walk between some farm buildings and out to a road. Go left, down the road, and cross the beck once again at **Morkin Bridge**.

④ Bear immediately right through a gate on to Yorkshire Water land and follow a good metalled track uphill. You can lengthen your stride

WHILE YOU'RE THERE ⓘ

Visit **Cliffe Castle Museum**, set in an attractive hillside park on Spring Gardens Lane. It was built in the 1880s as a mansion for a mill owner, and is now Keighley's museum, specialising in natural history and geology.

as the track traverses heather moorland, and passes a lonely farm, **Higher Intake**. The highest point of your walk is soon reached: **Keighley Moor Reservoir**.

⑤ Walk left, across the top of the dam. At the far end of the reservoir ignore the more obvious track to the right. Keep left of a concrete post to join a grassy moorland track, slightly downhill. The path becomes indistinct at a boggy section. Just keep straight ahead to meet a wall. Follow the wall for 150yds (138m) before going through a gateway in the wall. Bear half right to cross a line of grouse butts and locate a distinct but narrow path through the heather. Follow this path to a wall stile where you join a walled track heading right.

⑥ Follow this track, **Broad Head Lane**, soon leaving the moorland behind. The track is metalled once you reach an isolated group of houses. Cross a road by a farm and continue on a path to **Newsholme**.

⑦ Walk between houses on to a metalled lane, following it down to the next group of houses. Take a lane on your left, which soon becomes a track. Cross a beck and meet a road. Walk left down into **Goose Eye**. Walk through the village and steeply up the road. The road bends sharp right, then sharp left. Take a path to the right here, which delivers you back into **Laycock**.

WHERE TO EAT AND DRINK ⓘ

The **Turkey Inn**, towards the beginning of the walk in Goose Eye, is a splendid village pub, with a reputation for good food that extents much further afield.

Along the Colne Valley

The rural face of the valley between Slaithwaite and Marsden.

•**DISTANCE**•	6 miles (9.7km)
•**MINIMUM TIME**•	2hrs 30min
•**ASCENT / GRADIENT**•	550ft (170m) ▲▲▲
•**LEVEL OF DIFFICULTY**•	🚶🚶 🚶🚶 🚶
•**PATHS**•	Field paths, good tracks and canal tow path, 12 stiles
•**LANDSCAPE**•	Typical South Pennine country, canalside
•**SUGGESTED MAP**•	aqua3 OS Outdoor Leisure 21 South Pennines
•**START / FINISH**•	Grid reference: SE 079140
•**DOG FRIENDLINESS**•	Tow path is especially good for dogs
•**PARKING**•	Plenty of street parking in Slaithwaite
•**PUBLIC TOILETS**•	Slaithwaite and Marsden

BACKGROUND TO THE WALK

Transport across the Pennine watershed has always presented problems. The Leeds and Liverpool Canal, built during the 1770s, took a convoluted route across the Pennines, through the Aire Gap at Skipton. Then came the Rochdale Canal. However, its more direct route came at a high price: mile for mile, this canal has more locks than any other inland waterway in the country. With the increase in trade between Yorkshire and Lancashire, a third route across the Pennines was soon needed. The Huddersfield Narrow Canal links Huddersfield with Ashton-under-Lyne in Greater Manchester. Though only 20 miles long, it includes the Standedge Tunnel (▶ Walk 31). Begun in 1798, and dug with pick, shovel and dynamite, the canal was opened to traffic in 1811.

Beads on a String

The Colne Valley, to the west of Huddersfield, is representative of industrial West Yorkshire. Towns with evocative names – Milnsbridge, Linthwaite, Slaithwaite and Marsden – are threaded along the River Colne like beads on a string. In the 18th century this was a landscape of scattered farms and hand-loom weavers, mostly situated on the higher ground. As with Calderdale, a few miles to the north, the deep-cut valley of the Colne was transformed by the Industrial Revolution. Once the textile processes began to be mechanised, mills were built in the valley bottom by the new breed of industrial entrepreneurs. They specialised in the production of fine worsted cloth.

The River Colne provided the power for the first mills, and the canal subsequently improved the transport links. The mills grew larger as water power gave way to steam, towering over the rows of terraced houses built in their shadows. Throughout this walk you can see the mill chimneys and the saw-tooth roof-lines of the weaving sheds, though some mills are ruinous and others are now given over to other trades.

Slaithwaite (often pronounced 'Slowitt') is typical of the textile towns in the Colne Valley: unpretentious, a little bit scruffy. It looks to be an unlikely spa town. But that's what it became, albeit briefly, when its mineral springs were compared favourably with those of Harrogate. Slaithwaite is undergoing a face-lift; in particular, a filled-in section of the canal is being opened up, to enable water-borne traffic to be manoeuvred through the town.

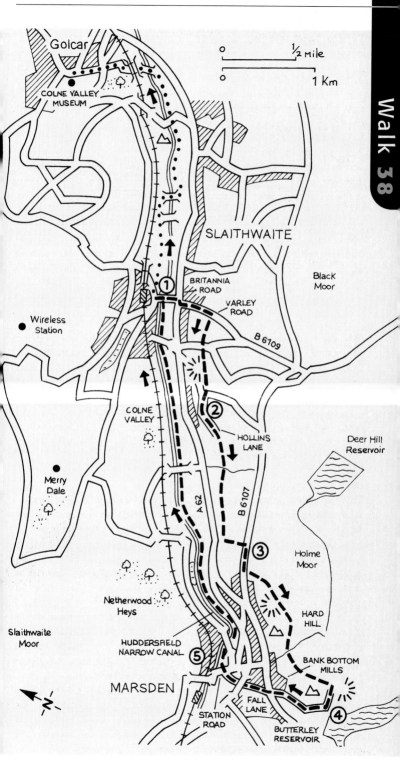

Walk 38

Walk 38 Directions

① Walk along **Britannia Road** up to the main A62 road. Cross over, turn right and take **Varley Road** up to the left. Beyond the last house go right, through a stile next to a gate. Join a grassy track across a field to a stile on the right-hand end of the wall ahead. Follow a wall to your right, across a stile, to a very minor road. Go right here, and follow the road left to a T-junction. Go straight ahead here, on a track; after just 20yds (18m) bear left on a track between houses. Squeeze past a gate on to a field path, with great views of the **Colne Valley**. Follow a wall on your right; towards its end go through a gap in the wall and take the steps, to continue in the same direction. After a step stile, keep to the right, slightly downhill, following a wall to another stile taking you on to a road.

② Go right, along the road, for 20yds (18m), then left on to a metalled track (signed 'Hollins Lane'). Continue as the track becomes rougher; when it peters out, keep left of an old cottage and go through a gate. Follow a field-edge path ahead, through a pair of gates either side of a beck. Pass a ruined house to descend on a walled path. When it bears sharp right keep straight ahead through a gate on to a field path. Follow a wall on your right; where it ends keep ahead, slightly uphill across two fields, and meet a walled track. Go left here, towards a farm. Go right, after 50yds (46m), through a stile and a pair of gates, on to another walled path downhill. The path soon bears right; take a stile to the left to follow a field-edge path. Cross another field and go left,

uphill, where you meet a wall. Take a stile and follow a walled path up to the B6107.

③ Go right, along the road, for just 75yds (68m), and take a stony track to your left. Keep left of a house, via a kissing gate, as you get good views across **Marsden** and the head of the **Colne Valley** (there are a number of paths that offer a more direct route down to **Marsden**, but you'll be missing out on the best views if you take a short-cut). About 150yds (138m) past the house bear right at a fork, taking the less obvious track. You soon follow a wall, beginning a slow descent. Across a beck, the track forks again; keep left, uphill, to skirt the shoulder of much-quarried **Hard Hill**. The track takes you steeply downhill, then up to a stile, then down again to cross a beck on a stone retaining wall. After another little climb, you have level walking and superb views, with **Butterley Reservoir** ahead of you. Bear left, steeply uphill, at a tiny stone building, cross two stiles and meet a track. Follow it right, downhill, to meet a road.

④ Go right, down the road, passing terraced houses dwarfed by **Bank Bottom Mills**. Keep straight ahead at the roundabout, down **Fall Lane**, soon bearing left to dip beneath the main road and into **Marsden**. Take **Station Road**, at the far end of a green, up to meet the **Huddersfield Narrow Canal**.

⑤ Take a path on the right that soon joins the canal tow path. Follow the canal for about 3 miles (4.8km) – passing beneath a road, past several locks and pools, between reservoirs, under two more road bridges – and eventually back into **Slaithwaite**.

Up the Ginnels to Golcar

An old hand-weaving village, still retaining its character on the outskirts of Huddersfield.

See map and information panel for Walk 38

•DISTANCE•	3 miles (4.8km)
•MINIMUM TIME•	2hrs 30min
•ASCENT / GRADIENT•	377ft (115m) ▲▲▲
•LEVEL OF DIFFICULTY•	🚶 🚶 🚶

Walk 39 Directions (Walk 38 option)

A short extension to Walk 38 can be made by continuing through **Slaithwaite**, still following the canal tow path. Beyond a derelict mill (and empty mill dam) you see another huge mill, also surplus to requirement, on your right. Pass a footbridge over the canal, but cross the next one, 150yds (138m) further on. Take steps, then a metalled path, steeply uphill. Ignore side-paths to walk beneath the double arch of a railway viaduct; at a fork of tracks keep left, uphill. Follow this track up into the hill village of **Golcar**.

Though only 3 miles (4.8km) from the centre of Huddersfield, the hilltop village of Golcar has managed to keep its identity. The village boasts a number of well-preserved hand-weavers' cottages, which provided living and working accommodation under one roof.

The top stories were typically south-facing, with long rows of mullioned windows allowing as much light as possible into the loom chambers. In 1970 three of these cottages were amalgamated to form the Colne Valley Museum. Here you can get a good impression of what life was like for weavers and their families, before the textile industries developed on a truly industrial scale, and production shifted from hilltop villages to the mill towns in the valley. There's a loom chamber, a weaver's living room and a gaslit clogger's shop. After investigating the ginnels, weavers' cottages and the **Colne Valley Museum**, retrace your steps down to the canal, and follow it back to **Slaithwaite**.

WHERE TO EAT AND DRINK ℹ️

You have a wide choice of pubs and cafés on this walk, in both Slaithwaite and Marsden. The **Railway**, close to the rail station and canal, in Marsden, comes at the halfway point of Walk 38.

WHAT TO LOOK FOR ℹ️

When Enoch and James Taylor of Marsden started manufacturing cropping frames, they caused consternation amongst the shearers, who feared for their livelihoods. They realised that a single machine could do the work of many men. So, banded together as 'Luddites', the shearers attacked the mills where the hated frames were being introduced. The **grave of Enoch Taylor** can be seen on Walk 38, on a small green you pass shortly after walking under the A62 and into Marsden.

Walk 40

A Stroll Through Judy Woods

Surrounded by towns these are some of the finest beech woods in West Yorkshire.

•DISTANCE•	3½ miles (5.7km)
•MINIMUM TIME•	1hr 30min
•ASCENT / GRADIENT•	328ft (100m) ▲ ▲ ▲
•LEVEL OF DIFFICULTY•	🚶 🚶 🚶
•PATHS•	Good tracks and woodland paths, 8 stiles
•LANDSCAPE•	Arable land and beech woods
•SUGGESTED MAP•	aqua3 OS explorer 288 Bradford & Huddersfield
•START / FINISH•	Grid reference: SE 147268
•DOG FRIENDLINESS•	Can be off lead in woods
•PARKING•	On Station Road (off the A641 at Wyke) near information panel and kissing gate giving access into Judy Woods
•PUBLIC TOILETS•	None on route

Walk 40 Directions

Judy Woods are hemmed in by Wyke, Hipperholme, Shelf, Wibsey, Stone Chair and other intriguingly named West Yorkshire towns. Nevertheless, these are some of the finest broadleaved woods in the county. You will look in vain for 'Judy Woods' on the Ordnance Survey map, as each spur of woodland bears a different name. But to locals the whole area is known as Judy Woods, recalling a woman called Judy North who lived here during the 19th century.

WHERE TO EAT AND DRINK 🛈
Now that Judy North no longer plies her trade there is nowhere on this short woodland walk that offers refreshments. On the A58, Whitehall Road, just heading out of Wyke near the start of the walk, you'll find the **Red Lion** serves real ales, bar meals and restaurant food in traditional surroundings.

Her cottage was near to Horse Close Bridge (usually known as Judy Bridge). She opened her gardens to the public, selling sweets and ginger beer to passers-by.

The geology of Judy Woods is defined by layers of coal over a bedrock of millstone grit. The coal has been mined for centuries, as is evidenced by the shallow depressions that can be seen during this walk. These are the remains of bell pits: an early and primitive method of opencast mining. A less obvious sign of local industry is the predominance of beech trees, which were probably planted during the reign of Queen Victoria. These trees are a colourful sight in autumn, when the leaves are turning from green to golden oranges, reds and yellows. But they were actually planted for a more prosaic purpose: to provide the raw materials for the manufacture of spindles and bobbins for the textile trades.

Walk through the kissing gate and follow the track ahead through these delightful beech woods. At a T-junction of tracks, go right, uphill, to leave the wood via a stile. Take the path ahead, on a little ridge, until you come to a wall and another track. Go left here and over two stiles to a surfaced lane. Turn right and follow the lane up to some houses.

Just past the first terraced houses bear left on an unadopted road, **Carr House Gate**, walking gradually uphill. Where the road ends, at a breaker's yard, keep straight ahead on a path which soon bears left at a transmitter and broadens into a track. At a T-junction of tracks, go right. This walled track takes you past **Park Dam**, down on the right. Bear right beyond **Royds Hall** but, after just 20yds (18m), take a step stile in the wall on your left.

Pass a Dutch barn on a path across the field, and cross a stile in a fence. Walk directly across the next field to a wall stile. Follow the wall on your right, skirting woodland and a housing estate. As you approach garden fences, you come to a cross-path. Go left here, and back into

Judy Wood via a metal kissing gate. Follow a broad track gradually downhill, with a steep slope to the right. When you approach a field, and a pylon, you have a choice of paths. Take either option; they both descend through the woods and meet up again at Judy Bridge.

Don't cross the bridge, but bear left, up a track. Almost immediately, take a gap stile in the wall to your right to access a footpath running parallel to the track. At the top of the slope, where the wall gives way to a metal fence, bear right. You have a choice of tracks here; take either of them, downhill, to leave the woods via a stile. Turn left to walk along **Station Road** back to your car.

> **WHAT TO LOOK FOR** ⓘ
>
> In the spring these beech woods are carpeted with **bluebells**. For most of the year these riotous flowers survive as tiny white bulbs about 6in (15cm) below the woodland floor. From late April until early June the succulent green stems rise up to as much as 18in (45cm) in height. The individual flowers are very similar to the flowers of the garden hyacinth, though the bluebell's scent is a little more subtle.

> **WHILE YOU'RE THERE** ⓘ
>
> This is the closest walk in the book to the centre of **Bradford**, offering a good opportunity to explore this bustling and metropolitan city. There is plenty to occupy your time here. The National Museum of Photography, Film and Television, opposite the Alhambra Theatre, has been expensively revamped. It's an excellent place to take the family, with the monstrous IMAX cinema screen being a particular attraction. Although much damaged by 1960s redevelopment, the city centre still has some fine architecture reflecting the heyday of the city's worsted trade which brought it great wealth. Particularly impressive is the town hall and the quarter known as Little Germany. The Colour Museum is a little-known gem, exploring the fascinating history, theory and technology behind many visual effects we take for granted. Newly opened, to reflect the city's proud multicultural heritage, is Life Force, the National Millennium Faith Experience.

Walk 41

Rishworth Moor's Expanse

A bracing ramble on old moorland tracks, with extensive views all the way.

•DISTANCE•	5½ miles (8.8km)
•MINIMUM TIME•	2hrs 30min
•ASCENT / GRADIENT•	328ft (100m) ▲▲▲
•LEVEL OF DIFFICULTY•	🚶 🚶 🚶
•PATHS•	Moorland paths; may be boggy after rain
•LANDSCAPE•	Open moorland
•SUGGESTED MAP•	aqua3 OS Outdoor Leisure 21 South Pennines
•START / FINISH•	Grid reference: SE 010184
•DOG FRIENDLINESS•	Under control where sheep are grazing
•PARKING•	Small car park above Baitings Reservoir
•PUBLIC TOILETS•	None on route

BACKGROUND TO THE WALK

The first part of this exhilarating moorland walk is called Blackstone Edge Road and was much used by quarrymen. The moorland is peaty, and the path may be boggy in places, so this walk is best tackled during a dry spell, when there is good visibility (both for ease of route-finding and to enjoy the views). The views are extensive. On the outward section of the walk, you can look down on the cars streaming along the M62, making easy work of traversing the Pennine watershed. You will see that the east- and west-bound carriageways divide around a solitary farm. The farmer's protests about the motorway being built – and this surreal diversion – were much in the news when the road was being constructed.

As you stride out across Rishworth Moor, probably sighting few other walkers, you can pity the motorists in their little metal boxes. Or, if the weather is turning nasty, you may feel a twinge of envy instead. On the second half of the walk you get excellent views of the Ryburn Valley and beyond, including Blackstone Edge, Pendle Hill and distant windfarms.

The M62 Motorway

The South Pennine hills, straddling the Yorkshire/Lancashire boundary and watershed, have long been a great obstacle to travel. A fascinating paved road climbs steeply up Blackstone Edge; opinions are divided as to whether it is Roman or a medieval packhorse track. But no one was in any doubt that this was difficult terrain. The redoubtable traveller, Celia Fiennes, coming this way in 1698, described this route as '...a dismal high precipice, steep in ascent'. Daniel Defoe came the same way in August 1724, during a blizzard that was unseasonal even for the Pennines.

A succession of turnpike roads were built in the 18th and early 19th centuries, which offered increasingly comfortable gradients. Yet it was as recently as the 1970s, with the building of the M62 motorway, that trans-Pennine travel finally became routine. Surveyors did some of their initial work using ponies: the easiest mode of transport in this bleak and inhospitable landscape. As drivers now cruise effortlessly across the empty moors, it's easy to forget just what a feat of engineering it was to build 'the motorway in the clouds'. At an altitude of 1,220ft (370m), the M62 is the highest motorway in the country, and this Pennine section offers some dramatic features. Scammonden Bridge, arching across a deep cutting, is the largest single-span bridge in Europe. Scammonden Reservoir was created by damming the Deanhead Valley, flooding a dozen farms in the process. The reservoir's huge dam, which also carries the motorway, is the largest earth-filled dam in Europe. It took five years to build the dam, and a further two years to fill with water. It may be easier to travel across the Pennines these days, but nature has a way of reminding us not to take things for granted. When it was opened, the M62 was called, somewhat optimistically, 'the motorway that never closes'. In fact, the weather up here is notoriously unpredictable, and few years pass without the traffic seizing up in winter's icy grip.

Walk 41

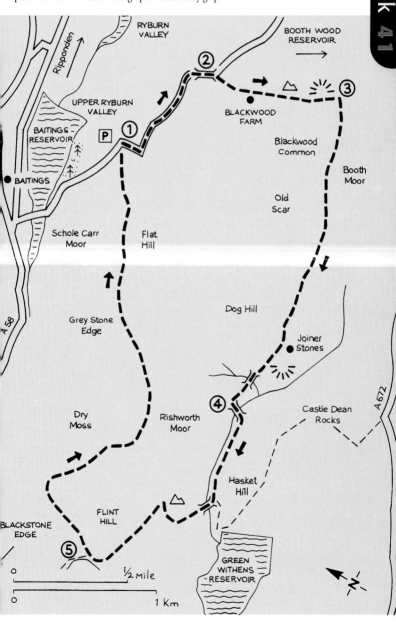

Walk 41

Walk 41 Directions

① From the car park, walk left down the road. 50yds (46m) after crossing the beck, take a gate in the wall on your right (signposted to **Booth Wood Reservoir**).

② Follow a tumbledown wall uphill towards the left-hand side of **Blackwood Farm**. Walk between the farmhouse and an outbuilding, to a gate at the top of the farmyard. Walk up the next field to a stile and continue steeply uphill, following the wall to your right. Look for views of the **Ryburn Valley**, as you crest the hill and arrive at a ladder stile, next to a gate in the wall.

③ From here you strike off to the right, across rough moorland; the path is distinct but narrow. Keep straight ahead at a yellow-topped post (you will see others on your route). Walk roughly parallel to the M62, heading just to the right of a tall mast on the far side of the motorway. At the next waymarker stick, bear slightly right, on a less obvious path. As you start to walk downhill you have good views down to **Green Withens Reservoir** ahead. Descend to cross a side-beck on a little plank bridge, to meet the reservoir drainage channel.

④ Take a bridge over the channel and walk right, following this watercourse towards the reservoir. About 300yds (274m) before the reservoir embankment, take a bridge back over the channel (waymarked '**Blackstone Edge and Baitings**'). Bear slightly left to follow a path uphill – soon quite steeply – before it levels out and bears left around **Flint Hill**. The view behind you recedes; ahead is the **Upper Ryburn Valley**. Descend to a water channel on your left and a fork of paths.

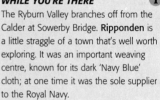

WHILE YOU'RE THERE
The Ryburn Valley branches off from the Calder at Sowerby Bridge. **Ripponden** is a little straggle of a town that's well worth exploring. It was an important weaving centre, known for its dark 'Navy Blue' cloth; at one time it was the sole supplier to the Royal Navy.

⑤ Go right here (a sign indicates **Baitings Reservoir**), continuing to skirt the hill on a good, level path. Keep left, where the path forks, to begin a gradual descent towards **Baitings Reservoir**. When you come to a wall corner, keep straight ahead, following the wall on your left. Soon you are on a walled track, passing through two gates and finally emerging at the little car park above the reservoir.

WHERE TO EAT AND DRINK
Take the opportunity to visit one of the oldest (14th-century) and most delightful pubs in West Yorkshire. You could drive through Ripponden without seeing it, because the **Old Bridge Inn** is tucked out of sight off the main A58 road. You'll find it near the church, on a cobbled lane, just beyond an old packhorse bridge. Real ale, picturesque surroundings and excellent food make the pub rather special.

WHAT TO LOOK FOR
The upland moors of the South Pennines are now officially recognised as important Sites of Special Scientific Interest (SSSI). It's a sparse landscape of heather, grasses, bilberry, cotton grass and crowberry, where birds such as the merlin and the golden plover still thrive. The only thing that's lacking, apart from trees, is people. You can stride out across these moors for mile after mile without seeing another walker.

Walk 42

Along Langfield Edge to Stoodley Pike

A classic South Pennine ridge walk to a much-loved landmark.

•DISTANCE•	7 miles (11.3km)
•MINIMUM TIME•	3hrs 30min
•ASCENT / GRADIENT•	1,017ft (310m) ▲▲▲
•LEVEL OF DIFFICULTY•	🏃 🏃 🏃
•PATHS•	Good paths and tracks, 3 stiles
•LANDSCAPE•	Open moorland
•SUGGESTED MAP•	aqua3 OS Outdoor Leisure 21 South Pennines
•START / FINISH•	Grid reference: SD 936242
•DOG FRIENDLINESS•	Under control as sheep present throughout
•PARKING•	Free parking in centre of Todmorden
•PUBLIC TOILETS•	By bus station intodmorden

BACKGROUND TO THE WALK

Todmorden – call it 'Tod' if you want to sound like a local – is a border town, standing at the junction of three valley routes. Before the town was included in the old West Riding, the Yorkshire/Lancashire border divided the town in two. Todmorden's splendid town hall, built in an unrestrained classical Greek style, reflects this dual personality. On top of the town hall are carved figures which represent, on one side, the Lancashire cotton trade, and, on the other side, Yorkshire agriculture and engineering.

Stoodley Pike

Stoodley Pike is a ubiquitous sight around the Calder Valley, an unmistakable landmark. It seems you only need to turn a corner, or crest a hill, and it appears on the horizon. West Yorkshire is full of monuments built on prominent outcrops, but few of them dominate the view in quite the way that Stoodley Pike does.

In 1814, a trio of patriotic Todmorden men convened in a local pub, the Golden Lion. Now that the Napoleonic War was over, they wanted to commemorate the peace with a suitably grand monument. So they organised a public subscription, and raised enough money to erect a monument, 1,476ft (450m) up on Langfield Edge, overlooking the town. Construction was halted, briefly, when Napoleon rallied his troops, and was not completed until the following year, when he was finally defeated at the Battle of Waterloo. This original monument was undone by the Pennine weather. Ironically, it collapsed in 1854, on the very day that the Crimean War broke out. Another group of local worthies came together (yes, at the Golden Lion again) to raise more money. So the Stoodley Pike we see today is Mark II: 131ft (40m) high and built to commemorate the ending of hostilities in the Crimea.

Stoodley Pike remains visible for almost every step of this exhilarating ridge walk. As well as being a favourite destination for local walkers, the Pike is visited by walkers on the the Pennine Way. Remember to pack a torch for this walk. By climbing a flight of unlit stone steps inside the monument, you emerge at a viewing platform offering panoramic views over Calderdale and beyond.

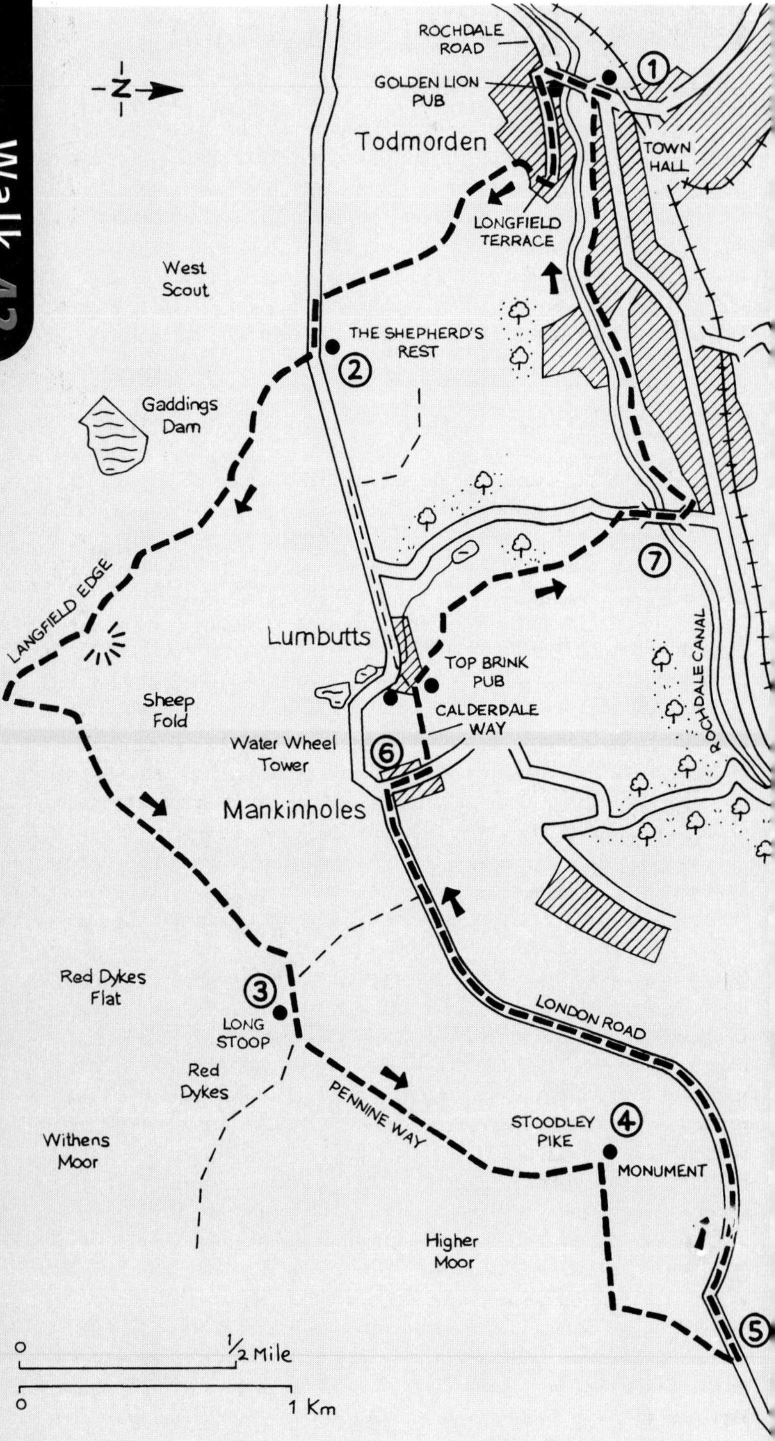
N
ROCHDALE ROAD
GOLDEN LION PUB
Todmorden
TOWN HALL
LONGFIELD TERRACE
West Scout
THE SHEPHERD'S REST
Gaddings Dam
LANGFIELD EDGE
Lumbutts
TOP BRINK PUB
CALDERDALE WAY
Sheep Fold
Water Wheel Tower
Mankinholes
ROCHDALE CANAL
Red Dykes Flat
LONG STOOP
Red Dykes
PENNINE WAY
LONDON ROAD
STOODLEY PIKE
MONUMENT
Withens Moor
Higher Moor
0
1/2 Mile
0
1 Km

Walk 42 Directions

① From the town hall in the centre of **Todmorden**, take the **Rochdale road** (A6033), cross the canal, and bear left immediately after the **Golden Lion** pub. Walk up the road and take the first road on the left, to avoid a housing estate. At the top of the hill the road peters out at **Longfield Terrace**. Take a track to the left, to find yourself suddenly 'on the tops'. When the track forks, keep left to a farm building, from where you will get the first glimpse of your destination – **Stoodley Pike** – on the horizon ahead. Continue along the farm track to a road. Go left, to find a pub, the **Shepherd's Rest,** in splendid isolation.

WHERE TO EAT AND DRINK ⓘ

Despite the rugged nature of this walk you have a choice of pubs. The isolated **Shepherd's Rest** is near the beginning, while the **Top Brink** in Lumbutts is towards the end. If you want to sit in the pub where the raising of Stoodley Pike was first discussed, you must wait till you have finished the walk: the **Golden Lion** is in Todmorden, close to the canal.

---

② Opposite the pub, take a track leading through a gate, uphill, onto **Langfield Common**. Keep left at old quarry workings, as the track narrows to a good path. Once you round the head of the clough keep right as the path forks, to follow the ridge top, **Langfield Edge,** with views of **Calderdale** to the left.

③ There is a meeting of paths by a waymarker stone known as **Long Stoop**. Continue straight ahead, crossing a superb paved causeway, on what is a section of the **Pennine Way**. You have level walking now until you reach **Stoodley Pike**.

④ Walk past the monument, as the path bears right, downhill, to a gap stile in a wall. After just 50yds (46m), take a ladder stile in an adjacent wall to the left. Continue downhill to meet a track. You leave the route of the **Pennine Way** here, by walking left along the wide and well-made track.

⑤ This track, known as **London Road**, offers a long but gentle descent to a road. Go right, into the hamlet of **Mankinholes**.

⑥ About 100yds (91m) beyond the last house, take a paved, walled track on the left, signed 'Calderdale Way', that emerges at the **Top Brink** pub in another tiny settlement, **Lumbutts**. Bear right to take a path between houses and follow a section of causeway on a path between a fence and a wall. At a gap stile in a wall, head right, slightly uphill, across a field to another gap stile. Your path now leads downhill through the steep-sided valley. Join a farm track, downhill, and meet a minor road by cottages. Go right, passing a derelict mill, to cross the **Rochdale Canal**.

⑦ Join the tow path to the left, to follow the canal back into the centre of **Todmorden**.

WHAT TO LOOK FOR ⓘ

London Road, the fancifully named track you follow from Stoodley Pike down into Mankinholes, was a 'cotton famine road'. When the cotton trade suffered one of its periodic slumps, mill owner John Fielden of Todmorden put some of his men to work on building this road, so he could ride his carriage up to Stoodley Pike. Fielden also built Dobroyd Castle, its castellated turrets looking slightly out of place on a hill overlooking the town. This is now a Buddhist retreat.

Hardcastle Crags & Crimsworth Dean

A pair of beautiful wooded valleys, linked by a high level path.

•DISTANCE•	5 miles (8km)
•MINIMUM TIME•	2hrs 30min
•ASCENT / GRADIENT•	787ft (240m) ▲▲▲
•LEVEL OF DIFFICULTY•	🚶🚶 🚶🚶 🚶
•PATHS•	Good paths and tracks, plus open pasture, no stiles
•LANDSCAPE•	Woodland, fields and moorland fringe
•SUGGESTED MAP•	aqua3 OS Outdoor Leisure 21 South Pennines
•START / FINISH•	Grid reference: SD 988291
•DOG FRIENDLINESS•	Plenty of opportunities for dogs to be off lead
•PARKING•	National Trust pay-and-display car parks at Midgehole, near Hebden Bridge (accessible via A6033, Keighley Road)
•PUBLIC TOILETS•	Near car park

BACKGROUND TO THE WALK

Hebden Bridge, just 4 miles (6.4km) from the Yorkshire/Lancashire border, has been a popular place to visit ever since the railway was extended across the Pennines, through the Calder Valley. But those train passengers weren't coming for a day out in a grimy little mill town; the big attraction was the wooded valley of Hebden Dale – usually called 'Hardcastle Crags' – just a short charabanc ride away. 'Hebden Bridge for Hardcastle Crags' was the stationmaster's cry, as trains approached the station. Here were shady woods, easy riverside walks and places to spread out a picnic blanket. To people who lived in the terraced streets of Bradford, Leeds or Halifax, Hardcastle Crags must have seemed idyllic. The steep-sided valley reminded Swiss visitors of their own country, and became 'Little Switzerland' – at least to the writers of tourist brochures. The only disappointment, in fact, was the crags themselves: unassuming gritstone outcrops, almost hidden by trees.

Industrial Demands

The Industrial Revolution created a huge demand for water: for mills, factories and domestic use. To quench the thirst of the rapidly expanding textile towns, many steep-sided valleys, known in the South Pennines as cloughs, were dammed to create reservoirs. Six of these lie within easy walking distance of Hardcastle Crags. They represented huge feats of civil engineering by the hundreds of navvies who built them, around the end of the 19th century, with picks and shovels. The men were housed in a shanty town, known as Dawson City and both men and materials were transported to the work-sites by a convoluted steam-powered railway system that crossed the valley on an elaborate wooden viaduct.

Hardcastle Crags escaped the indignity of being turned into a reservoir, but it was touch and go. Three times during the last 50 years (the last time was in 1970) plans were drawn up to flood the valley. And three times, thankfully, wiser counsels prevailed and the plans were turned down. Lord Savile, a major landowner in the area, once owned the valley. It was he who supplemented the natural woodland with plantings of new trees –

particularly pines, and laid out the walks and the carriage drive. In 1948 Lord Savile donated Hardcastle Crags, and the nearby valley of Crimsworth Dean, to the National Trust. Because of this bequeathment, the future of this delightful valley looks secure and local people will continue to enjoy this valuable amenity.

Hardcastle Crags are a haven for wildlife. Bird watchers can look out for pied flycatchers, woodpeckers, jays, sparrowhawks and the ubiquitous dipper – which never strays from the environs of Hebden Water. In spring there are displays of bluebells; in summer the woods are filled with bird-song; the beech woods are a riot of colour as the leaves turn each autumn.

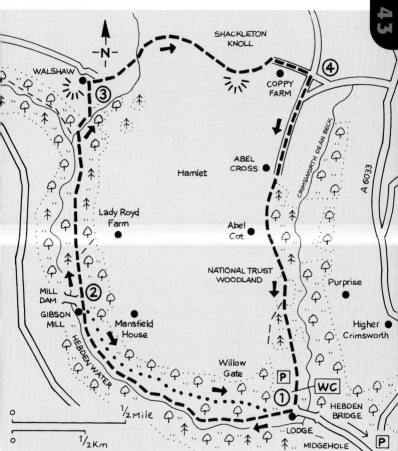

Walk 43 Directions

① Walk up the drive, passing the lodge, and into the woods. Take the first path to the left, which descends to **Hebden Water**. Follow a good riverside path through delectable woodland, passing **Hebden Hey** –

a popular picnic site, with stepping stones – to reach **Gibson Mill**. The buildings, and mill dam behind, are worth investigating.

② For this longer walk you join the track uphill, to the right of **Gibson Mill**, soon passing the crags that give the woods their name.

Walk 43

Keep on the main track, ignoring side-paths, to leave woodland and meet a metalled road. Keep left here, still uphill, across a beck and approach **Walshaw**, a knot of houses enjoying terrific views.

③ Just before you reach the houses – when you are opposite some barns – bear sharp right through a gate onto an enclosed track (signed to **Crimsworth Dean**). You are soon on a grassy track across pasture, descending to a beck and through a gate. Walk uphill, soon bearing to the right as you follow a wall around the shoulder of **Shackleton Hill**. Go through a gate in the wall on your left, and continue as the path bears right, still following the wall, but now it's on your right. Here you have level walking and great views. Take a gate in a wall on the right, just above **Coppy Farm**, to join a walled track downhill into the valley of

Crimsworth Dean. You meet a more substantial track by another ruin of a farm. This track is the old road from **Hebden Bridge** to **Haworth**: a great walk to contemplate for another day.

④ Bear right, along this elevated track, passing a farm on the left. Look out, by a farm access track to the right, for **Abel Cross**: not one but a pair of old waymarker stones. Continue down the main track, into National Trust woodland, keeping left, after a field, when the track forks. Beyond a pair of cottages the track is metalled; you soon arrive back at the car parks at **Midgehole**.

Hebden Water & Gibson Mill

One of the finest woodland walks in West Yorkshire.
See map and information panel for Walk 43

•DISTANCE•	2½ miles (4km)
•MINIMUM TIME•	1hr 30min
•ASCENT / GRADIENT•	66ft (20m) ▲ ▲▲
•LEVEL OF DIFFICULTY•	🚶🚶 🚶🚶 🚶🚶

Walk 44 Directions (Walk 43 option)

If you only have time to walk to Gibson Mill and back, you will have enjoyed arguably the finest short woodland walk in West Yorkshire. The mill was built 200 years ago, when Hebden Water was harnessed to turn a waterwheel and power the cotton spinning machines. The mill pond, behind the mill itself, was built to maintain a good supply of water, even when the river levels were low. This was not the only mill in the valley, but it's the only one still standing. Gibson Mill itself occupies a romantic setting, deep in the woods, its image reflected in the adjacent mill pond. But appearances can be deceptive.

The mill was notorious for its poor working conditions. From a report of 1833 we learn that the 22 employees in Gibson Mill were accustomed to a 72-hour week, with children as young as 10 starting their working day at 6AM and finishing at 7:30PM. Because of their size the children were able to make repairs to the machines while they were still running. Accidents were common. The children had just two breaks during their day – for breakfast and dinner. It wasn't until 1847 that legislation was passed, to limit the working day for women and children to 'only' ten hours. The waterwheel stopped turning in 1852, when the mill was converted to steam power. But by the 1890s the mill had become redundant. Due to its attractive situation, however, it was put to a variety of recreational uses. At various times up to the Second World War, it was a tea room, dance hall, dining saloon, even a roller skating rink. The mill pond became a rowing lake. The National Trust now has plans to restore the building into an environmental centre.

Follow the track from the car park at **Midgeley**, up into the woods. Take the first path on the left, after the gatehouse, down to accompany **Hebden Water** upstream. Follow the riverside path passing **Hebden Hey,** a popular picnic site, and two more sets of stepping stones before you arrive at **Gibson Mill**.

Many good paths and tracks converge here, and all provide excellent walking. But for this short ramble you should join the sandy track (known as the carriage drive) that passes the mill. Walk to the right, still through woodland, as the track leads you back to the car park.

East Riddlesden Hall

An opportunity to visit one of West Yorkshire's finest 'Halifax' houses.

•DISTANCE•	4 miles (6.4km)
•MINIMUM TIME•	2hrs
•ASCENT / GRADIENT•	426ft (120m) ▲▲ ▲▲
•LEVEL OF DIFFICULTY•	🚶🚶 🚶 🚶
•PATHS•	Field paths and canal tow path, 8 stiles
•LANDSCAPE•	Arable landscape and canalside
•SUGGESTED MAP•	aqua3 OS Explorer 297 Lower Wharfedale
•START / FINISH•	Grid reference: SE 099420
•DOG FRIENDLINESS•	Good on walk, but not permitted in Hall
•PARKING•	Lay-bys in East Morton
•PUBLIC TOILETS•	East Morton

Walk 45 Directions

Now hidden away in the suburbs of Keighley, East Riddlesden Hall is one of West Yorkshire's architectural gems. This gaunt, gritstone manor house was built in the 1640s by James Murgatroyd, a wealthy yeoman clothier from Halifax. It was built on the site of an even older hall, but of this earlier building only the central hall remains. Above the battlements of the hall's bothy, James Murgatroyd had two heads carved in stone – a bewigged Charles I and his queen – with the legend 'Vive le Roy' (long live the king). James and his family were staunch royalists during the

Civil War, in a time and place when it was unwise to advertise such allegiance. Many royalists were forced to forfeit their land, an indignity from which the Murgatroyds were spared. But the family's loyalties did bring trouble elsewhere. Another of Murgatroyd's houses, The Hollins at Warley near Halifax, was being used to store Royalist arms when it was attacked by Parliamentary troops. Despite a fierce battle in which the defenders even tore off the roof slates to throw at their assailants, the house was taken along with 44 prisoners. James and his family must have escaped, or at least were released, and by 1648 East Riddlesden Hall was completed.

Though surrounded by houses today, East Riddlesden Hall used to be a farm. The huge tithe barn is one of the finest examples in the North of England, and a watermill once stood by the nearby River Aire. The fishpond at the front of the house may have been made by monks from Bolton Abbey. During the 18th and 19th centuries it was

---

WHILE YOU'RE THERE ⓘ

As well as visiting the National Trust's **East Riddlesden Hall**, which forms the theme for this walk, take a little time to explore the neighbouring mill town of **Keighley** (say 'Keith-lee'). There are still some fine Victorian buildings intact which give an indication of the wealth the textile industry brought with it. There is also an excellent indoor market.

> ### WHERE TO EAT AND DRINK
> The **Busfeild Arms** (named after a prominent local family), at the start of the walk in East Morton, offers good food, if eccentric spelling. The **Marquis of Granby**, just over the canal from East Riddlesden Hall, offers refreshments at the half-way point.

let by tenant farmers. This accounts for the fact that the hall has stayed substantially unaltered, retaining many of its original features. The most recent change of ownership left the hall in the stewardship of the National Trust.

The rose windows, over the entrance porches at the front and back of the hall, are typical of the 'Halifax' houses in the South Pennines. With its oak-panelled rooms and mullioned windows, the hall provides a sympathetic setting for collections of domestic utensils and Yorkshire oak furniture dating from the 17th and 18th centuries. In the great barn, 130ft (40m) long, are displays of farm carts and tools and the walled gardens, at the back of the hall, are being restored.

Walk uphill, past the **Busfeild Arms** (this is the correct spelling!), for 150yds (138m). As the road descends, take cobbled **Little Lane**, to your right. Walk past houses to a gate; it gives access to a walled path descending to a road. Go right and immediately left, down **Hawthorne Way**. When this cul-de-sac ends, at a house, take a stile ahead onto a field path. Follow a wall until it bears to the right, then keep straight ahead, down to a stile at the bottom of the field. A path descends, between fences, to a stile in a wall. Turn left when you reach the road, cross the **Leeds and Liverpool Canal** on a swing bridge, and go

right, along the canal tow path. Pass beneath a stone bridge. When you get to another swing bridge, leave the canal, and walk left, down the road. Cross the B6265 at the traffic lights, to enter the grounds of **East Riddlesden Hall**.

Having investigated the hall, retrace your steps to the canal and cross it on the swing bridge. Take the road (**Hospital Road**) immediately on the right, in front of the **Marquis of Granby** pub. This road ends at the gateposts of what was once a hospital. Take a path just to the left of them, onto a path between a wall and a fence. After 200yds (183m), when the path turns slightly to the right, look for a gap stile in the wall to your left. Walk uphill to another stile at the top-right corner of this long field. A grassy farm track continues uphill, bearing right to pass a farm and row of cottages in West Morton.

The track soon forks. Go left, still uphill, on a walled track which soon meets a road. Walk right, down the road for 200yds (183m). Where the road bends right, around a cricket pitch, take a gate on the left to follow a field path by a wall. Though the footpath itself is indistinct, continue in the same direction over stiles and two more fields to meet a walled path, which soon approaches **Moorlands Farm**. Join the farm's access track and walk down to a road. Go right here, past some cottages and back into **East Morton**.

> ### WHAT TO LOOK FOR ⓘ
> East Riddlesden Hall is blessed with a cast of ghostly characters. The most famous is the Grey Lady, the wife of a previous lord of the manor, seen wandering from room to room.

Walk 46

On the Packhorse Trail Along Salter Rake

An invigorating moorland walk, punctuated by reservoirs, finishing off with a stretch of the Rochdale Canal.

·DISTANCE·	5 miles (8km)
·MINIMUM TIME·	2hrs 30min
·ASCENT / GRADIENT·	656ft (200m) ▲▲ ▲▲ ▲
·LEVEL OF DIFFICULTY·	🏃 🏃 🏃
·PATHS·	Good paths and tracks throughout, 2 stiles
·LANDSCAPE·	Open moorland, reservoirs and canalside
·SUGGESTED MAP·	aqua3 OS Outdoor Leisure 21 South Pennines
·START / FINISH·	Grid reference: SD 945201
·DOG FRIENDLINESS·	Under control around sheep loose on open moorland
·PARKING·	At pull-in for cars at roadside, near Bird i' th' Hand pub on A6033, between Todmorden and Littleborough
·PUBLIC TOILETS·	None on route

BACKGROUND TO THE WALK

Salter Rake is an old packhorse road which, as the name suggests, was used particularly for transporting salt from the Cheshire salt mines across the Pennines. When these trading routes were first established, the Calder Valley was largely undrained. The teams of packhorse ponies, laden with pannier bags, would keep to the drier high ground, only descending into the valleys to cross rivers on the narrow stone bridges that are so typical of the area. Most of these causeways (or 'causeys') were paved with stones. More than three centuries after they were laid, these stones still fit snugly together as the pieces of a jigsaw. To judge from the way they are deeply 'dished', the stones have seen heavy use by countless horses' hooves.

Familiar Rocks

Gritstone rocks and outcrops are familiar features throughout the South Pennines. The Basin Stone, an oddly-shaped rock looks – from one viewpoint, at least – like a fish-tail. It is a prominent landmark high on Walsden Moor and was one of the many sites, well away from the watchful eyes of the authorities, used by travelling Methodist preachers when they delivered their open-air sermons.

Reservoirs

Like many of the reservoirs you will encounter whilst walking in the South Pennines, the trio you see from this walk – Warland, Light Hazzles and White Holme – were built to supply water for a canal. The Rochdale Canal was built to link Manchester to the Calder and Hebble Navigation at Sowerby Bridge. By the 1920s there was very little commercial traffic still using it, so the reservoirs were converted to an alternative use and joined the complex of water supply systems built to slake the thirst of East Lancashire's mill towns.

Walk 46

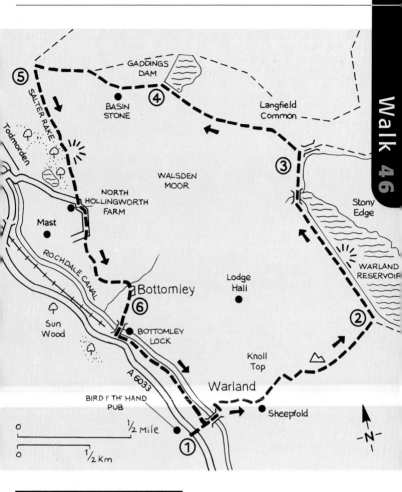

Walk 46 **Directions**

① Walk to the right along the road for just 75yds (68m). Cross the road and take a track on the left, **Warland Gate End,** past some cottages. Cross the **Rochdale Canal** on a swing bridge and follow the track uphill, between houses. At a sharp right-hand bend, by more houses, the track becomes metalled. Continue uphill, passing a house and stables, to a small gate above the house. From here you bear slightly right, up to another stile. Follow the wall to your left (which soon becomes a fence) with a

stream to your right. Cross the stream by a gate; you are now on land owned by United Utilities (formerly North West Water). As you approach the retaining wall of **Warland Reservoir**, you can follow the track on your right (or take a steeper short cut on the left) up to a track that follows the contours of the reservoir.

② Walk left along this good, level track, with terrific views over **Calderdale** and **East Lancashire**. Cross a bridge at the northern end of the reservoir, and keep on the track as it follows a drainage channel. When both track and channel wheel to the right, go left at a stone bridge, to follow a path (not very distinct and may be boggy) in the direction of another, smaller reservoir, with a windfarm visible on the horizon.

③ A line of paving stones will help to keep you dry-shod, before you walk along the left edge of **Gaddings Dam**.

④ Bear half left at the far end of the reservoir, by a set of stone steps, on a clear path that soon passes close to the curiously-shaped outcrop called the **Basin Stone**. Soon you come to a meeting of paths, marked with a small waymarker post.

⑤ Bear left here, on a path that's soon delineated by causeway stones; you are now following **Salter Rake**, an old packhouse road. Enjoy excellent views over **Walsden** as you make a gradual descent, still across open moorland, then accompanying a wall.

On approaching houses, go through a gate and between walls to join a metalled track past the houses and downhill. After 75yds (68m) you have a choice of routes. Keep left on a metalled track to another house. Through a metal gate below the house, follow the causeway stones to the right, accompanying a wall

---

WHAT TO LOOK FOR ⓘ

Steanor Bottom tollhouse is a small hexagonal building dating from the 1820s. You will find it on the main A6033 road, at a junction with a minor road, to the south of the Bird i' th' Hand pub. Tolls were collected here from any travellers wishing to use the new turnpike road. The tollhouse has been restored and retains its notice board presenting the tariff for all the different kinds of traffic, from sheep to carts.

(ignoring a more obvious track to the left). The footpath becomes sunken, between walls, as you descend and pass to the left of a white-painted house. The paved path takes you across a little beck and up into a small collection of houses, known as **Bottomley**. Go right here, down a metalled track, and bear immediately right again, through a gate, and on to a cobbled, walled path directly downhill, which takes you to the **Rochdale Canal**.

⑥ Cross the canal by the side of **Bottomley Lock**, and walk along the canal tow path. The fourth bridge you come to is the swing bridge. Go right here and back to the **Bird i' th' Hand** pub.

WHILE YOU'RE THERE ⓘ

South-east of Walsden, just off the A68 is a short, steep track over the Pennine watershed of **Blackstone Edge**. This elaborately paved path, about 13ft (4m) wide and with a stone channel down the middle, is marked on the Ordnance Survey map as a Roman road, but opinions about its origins are divided. It doesn't resemble other known roads of that period. Nor, however, is it like the paved packhorse causeways that criss-cross the South Pennines. One thing is sure: if it is Roman, it's one of the best-preserved examples in the country.

WHERE TO EAT AND DRINK ⓘ

Your one source of refreshment on this walk is the **Bird i' th' Hand** pub, where you park your car. It was built around 1825 to exploit the traffic using the turnpike road that had been opened just four years earlier. It's a homely, unpretentious locals' pub with a wide choice of lunchtime food, and is, of course, worth two in the bush...

The Bridestone Rocks from Lydgate

Ancient tracks and gritstone outcrops, with terrific views of the steep-sided Cliviger Valley.

•DISTANCE•	5 miles (8km)
•MINIMUM TIME•	2hrs 30min
•ASCENT / GRADIENT•	984ft (300m) ▲▲▲
•LEVEL OF DIFFICULTY•	🚶 🚶 🚶
•PATHS•	Moorland and packhorse paths, some quiet roads, 3 stiles
•LANDSCAPE•	Steep-sided valley and open moorland
•SUGGESTED MAP•	aqua3 OS Outdoor Leisure 21 South Pennines
•START / FINISH•	Grid reference: SD 924256
•DOG FRIENDLINESS•	Be careful around sheep grazing on the moorland
•PARKING•	Roadside parking in Lydgate, 1½ miles (2.4km) out of Todmorden, on A646, signposted to Burnley
•PUBLIC TOILETS•	None on route

BACKGROUND TO THE WALK

The Long Causeway, between Halifax and Burnley, is an ancient trading route, possibly dating back to the Bronze Age. Crosses and waymarker stones helped to guide travellers across the moorland wastes, though most of them have been lost or damaged in the intervening years. Amazingly, Mount Cross has survived intact: a splendid, though crudely carved, example of the Celtic 'wheel-head' design. Opinions differ about its age but it is certainly the oldest man-made artefact in the area, erected at least a thousand years ago.

The Sportsman's Inn, visited on this walk, is one of many isolated pubs in the South Pennines that seem to be situated 'miles from anywhere'. In fact they were built on old routes, and catered for customers on the move, such as drovers and the men who led the trains of packhorse ponies across the moorland tracks. The Sportsman's Inn lies on the Long Causeway, now upgraded to a high-level road between Todmorden and Burnley. These days the pub caters for motorists and walkers, with good food and beers.

The Bridestones

The hills and moors to the north of Todmorden are dotted with gritstone outcrops. The impressive piles of Orchan Rocks and Whirlaw Rocks are both encountered on this walk. But the most intriguing rock formations are to be found at the Bridestones. One rock in particular has been weathered by wind and water into a tear-drop shape, and stands on a base that looks far too slender to support its great weight. It resembles a rock in the North York Moors National Park, which is also known as the Bridestone.

Cliviger Valley

The Cliviger Valley links two towns – Todmorden in West Yorkshire and Burnley in Lancashire – that expanded with the textile trade, and then suffered when that trade went into decline. The valley itself is narrow and steep-sided, in places almost a gorge. Into the cramped confines of the valley are shoe-horned the road, railway line, the infant River Calder and communities such as Portsmouth, Cornholme and Lydgate that grew up around the textile mills. The mills were powered by fast-flowing becks, running off the steep hillsides. The valley is almost a microcosm of the Industrial Revolution: by no means beautiful, but full of character. This area is particularly well provided with good footpaths, some of them still paved with their original causey stones.

Walk 47 **Directions**

① From the post office in **Lydgate**, take **Church Road**. At the end go right, down the drive towards a house. Look immediately for a path that passes to the right of this house and soon goes beneath the arch of a railway viaduct. Join a stony track, as you walk steeply uphill, the track is sunken, between walls. Where the

walls end, the track gives access to open moorland. Keep right, along a track towards a farm. Keep left of the farmhouse, continuing along a walled track uphill. When you meet another walled track, go right towards a rocky outcrop on the first horizon. Beyond two gates you are on open moorland again: **Whirlaw Common**. Cross pasture on a section of paved causeway to arrive, via a gate, at **Whirlaw Stones**.

Walk 47

② Keep to the causeway that bears right, below the stones, with panoramic views of the **Cliviger Valley**, **Todmorden** and, ahead, **Stoodley Pike**. Leave **Whirlaw Common** by a gate on to a walled path. Bear sharp left at a farm, on a stony track that follows a wall uphill. Bear right around the rocks, to join **Windy Harbour Lane**. You have a steep climb, before the road levels off to meet **Eastwood Road**. Go left here for just 150yds (140m). Where the wall ends, take a stile on the left. A grassy path leads you to another fascinating collection of rocks, known as the **Bridestones**.

③ Continue past the **Bridestones** through a landscape of scattered boulders, before turning right to follow an indistinct path across rough terrain. When you meet a road, you'll be greeted by the sight of the **Sportsman's Inn**.

④ Go left, along the road; you have a mile (1.6km) of level walking, passing the **Hawks Stones** on the right and a handful of houses, until

you come to a minor road on the left. This is **Mount Lane**, signed to **Shore** and **Todmorden**. Walk down this road and beyond a farm on the right, take a good track to the left, slightly downhill. Look out for **Mount Cross** in a field to your left.

⑤ Detour past **Lower Intake Farm** on a path, soon enclosed by walls. 200yds (183m) beyond a small bridge over a stream, look out for a stile on your right, by a gate between heavy stone gateposts. Follow a field path downhill, keeping a wall to your left. This grassy track takes you beneath another gritstone outcrop, known as **Orchan Rocks**.

⑥ Where the wall bears left, beyond the rocks, follow it downhill to a stile. You now join a farm track that takes a serpentine route downhill, through woodland. Your way is clear: down into the valley and back into **Lydgate**.

Jumble Hole and Colden Clough

Textile history from cottage industry to the mills of bustling Hebden Bridge.

•DISTANCE•	5½ miles (8.8km)
•MINIMUM TIME•	3hrs
•ASCENT / GRADIENT•	722ft (220m) ▲▲▲
•LEVEL OF DIFFICULTY•	秀秀 秀秀 秀秀
•PATHS•	Good paths, 13 stiles
•LANDSCAPE•	Steep-sided valleys, fields and woodland
•SUGGESTED MAP•	aqua3 OS Outdoor Leisure 21 South Pennines
•START / FINISH•	Grid reference: SD 992272
•DOG FRIENDLINESS•	Good most of the way, but livestock in upland fields
•PARKING•	Pay-and-display car parks in Hebden Bridge
•PUBLIC TOILETS•	Hebden Bridge and Heptonstall

BACKGROUND TO THE WALK

This walk links the little town of Hebden Bridge with the old hand-weaving village of Heptonstall, using sections of a waymarked walk, the Calderdale Way. The hill village of Heptonstall is by far the older settlement and was, in its time, an important centre of the textile trade. A cursory look at a map shows Heptonstall to be at the hub of a complex network of old trackways, mostly used by packhorse trains carrying wool and cotton. And Heptonstall's Cloth Hall, where cloth was bought and sold, dates back to the 16th century. At this time Hebden Bridge was little more than a river crossing on an old packhorse causey.

Wheels of Industry

Heptonstall's importance came at the time when textiles were, literally, a cottage industry, with spinning and weaving being undertaken in isolated farmhouses. When the processes began to be mechanised, during the Industrial Revolution, Heptonstall, with no running water to power the waterwheels, was left high and dry. As soon as spinning and weaving developed on a truly industrial scale, communities sprang up wherever there was a ready supply of running water. So the town of Hebden Bridge was established in the valley, at the meeting of two rivers: the Calder and Hebden Water. The handsome 16th-century packhorse bridge that gives the town its name still spans Hebden Water.

At one time there were more than 30 mills in Hebden Bridge, their tall chimneys belching thick smoke into the Calder Valley. It used to be said that the only time you could see the town from the surrounding hills was during Wakes Week, the mill-hands' traditional holiday. The town's speciality was cotton: mostly hard-wearing fustian and corduroy. With Hebden Bridge being hemmed in by hills, and the mills occupying much of the available land on the valley bottom, the workers' houses had to be built up the steep slopes. An ingenious solution to the problem was to build 'top and bottom' houses, one dwelling on top of another. They can be viewed to best effect on the last leg of the walk, which offers a stunning birds-eye view over the town. Few looms clatter today and Hebden Bridge has reinvented itself as the 'capital' of Upper Calderdale, as a place to enjoy a day out. The town is known for its excellent walking country, bohemian population, trips along the Rochdale Canal by horse-drawn narrowboats and its summer arts festival. Jumble Hole Clough is a typical South Pennine steep-sided, wooded valley. Though a tranquil scene today, this little valley was once a centre of industry, with four mills exploiting the fast-flowing beck as it makes its way down to join the River Calder. You can see remains of all these mills, and some of their mill ponds, on this walk; but the most intriguing relic is Staups Mill, now an evocative ruin, near the top of Jumble Hole Clough.

Walk 48

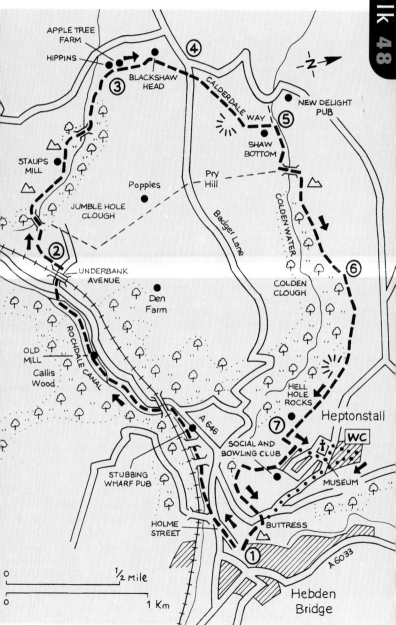

Walk 48 **Directions**

① From the centre of **Hebden Bridge**, walk along **Holme Street** to the **Rochdale Canal**. Go right to follow the tow path beneath two bridges, past the **Stubbing Wharf** pub and beneath a railway bridge. Beyond the bridge the canal broadens; 200yds (183m) further on and before the next bridge, bear right and join a track right, to the A646.

② Cross the road and bear right for just 75yds (68m) to take **Underbank Avenue**, on the left, through an arch. Bear left again, past houses, to where another road comes through the viaduct. Go right on a track past a mill, and follow the beck up into the woodland of **Jumble Hole Clough**. Beyond a ruined mill, leave the track and bear left to cross the beck. Beyond a hairpin bend, climb steeply, passing a dam. When the track wheels left, keep ahead, now above the beck. Take a gate and cross the bottom of a field, to re-enter woodland. Keep ahead uphill, to a gap in a fence. Walk downhill, past the ruins of **Staups Mill**, then steeply up to cross a bridge. Take steps and cross a field to a waymark. Keep left, following a wall to a gate in front of **Hippins**.

③ Join the **Calderdale Way**, bearing right up a track between farm buildings to a stile. Follow a path to the next stile; then between a fence and a wall. Cross the track to **Apple Tree Farm**, to follow a line of causeway stones across three more stiles, passing to the right of a cottage. Cross the field to a gate at the right corner, then follow a causeway over a stile, and along a track to **Blackshaw Head**.

④ Go right, along the road, for 20yds (18m), to take a gate on the left. Bear half right across the field to a stile, then follow the right edge of the next field. Cross four more fields, and stiles, to a gate. Go left down a path, to **Shaw Bottom**. Keep left of the house to a metalled track.

⑤ Go right, along the track (or left for the **New Delight** pub). When the track bears left, keep ahead on a stony track. Look out for a small marker post; go left here, steeply down steps, and cross **Colden Water** on a stone bridge. Climb up the other side, to follow a causeway to the right, at the top of woodland. At the second stile bear slightly left to keep following the causeway stones; your route is clear, through gates and stiles, as **Heptonstall** comes into view. Keep right at a crossing of tracks, passing to the left of a house. Keep straight ahead, on a walled path downhill, at the next crossing of tracks, by a bench. Keep left at the next fork to meet a road.

⑥ Go left here, uphill; just before the road bears left, take a gap in the wall to the right. From here your path meanders through woodland (it's a bit of a scramble in places). Emerge from the woodland, and follow a wall to **Hell Hole Rocks**.

⑦ Bear left at a wall-end, and cross an access road. At the junction turn right to the **Social and Bowling Club** (straight on for Walk 49). Go right, on a walled path and follow the wall to your left, downhill, soon through a spur of woodland and on to a track round to the left. Past houses you come to a road junction. Go left for 50yds (46m) and take the paved track right. This is the **Buttress**, taking you steeply down into **Hebden Bridge**.

On to Heptonstall

Extend your walk round Colden Clough to take in this famous hilltop village.
See map and information panel for Walk 48

•DISTANCE•	6 miles (9.7km)
•MINIMUM TIME•	4hrs
•ASCENT / GRADIENT•	722ft (220m) ▲▲▲
•LEVEL OF DIFFICULTY•	🚶🚶🚶

Walk 49 Directions (Walk 48 option)

If you extend Walk 49 with a look around **Heptonstall**, you won't be disappointed. It's a gem. Allow an hour or more to explore and soak up its unique atmosphere.

Go straight ahead at the junction after Point ⑦ to enter the village. The gritstone houses huddle closely together, as though sheltering from the prevailing wind; the effect is captivating. The old heart of Heptonstall is now a conservation area: a splendid example of a pre-industrial hill village. While Haworth sold its soul to the tourist trade, Heptonstall remains handsomely authentic.

The country's oldest Methodist Chapel in continuous use dates back to 1764. It was built to specifications laid down by John Wesley himself, who preached here on a number of occasions. He chose the octagonal shape because it offered 'no corner in which the devil can hide'. The old churchyard is paved with gravestones. It is shared, almost uniquely, by two churches: a capacious Victorian edifice and the ruins of the old medieval church. This is the resting place of David Hartley, King of the Coiners, who was hanged in 1779 for his part in the illegal 'clipping' of gold coins. The grave of Sylvia Plath, in the new graveyard, has become a shrine for lovers of her brittle, brilliant poetry.

Look too for the **Old Grammar School** (now a museum), the **Old Cloth Hall** and the cobbled main street. In **Weavers Square**, every Good Friday, the Pace Egg Play is performed by local players. It's a rumbustious tale of good against evil, its origins lost in time.

Having investigated Heptonstall, follow the cobbled main street downhill. Look out for a paved path on the left, accessed via a stile. Go right, at a road, past houses, to take the steep, packhorse road, known as the **Buttress,** back into **Hebden Bridge**.

> ### WHERE TO EAT AND DRINK   ⓘ
> The **New Delight** is conveniently situated at the halfway point of the walk. Good beer, imaginative food and stone-flagged floors make it the ideal spot for lunch. And, if the urge to continue walking deserts you, you can pick up a little country bus outside the door that will take you back to Hebden Bridge via the cobbled street of Heptonstall.

The Broadleaved Woodlands of Harden Beck

A short but entrancing woodland walk between Bradford and Bingley, to a splendid waterfall.

•DISTANCE•	3 miles (4.8km)
•MINIMUM TIME•	1hr 30min
•ASCENT / GRADIENT•	98ft (30m)
•LEVEL OF DIFFICULTY•	
•PATHS•	Woodland paths and tracks, and field paths, 6 stiles
•LANDSCAPE•	Deciduous woodland and arable land
•SUGGESTED MAP•	aqua3 OS Explorer 288 Bradford & Huddersfield, Outdoor Leisure 21 South Pennines
•START / FINISH•	Grid reference: SE 088378 (on Explorer 288)
•DOG FRIENDLINESS•	Can be off lead in woodland
•PARKING•	From Harden, take Wilsden Road to roadside parking at bottom of hill, just before bridge and Malt Shovel pub
•PUBLIC TOILETS•	None on route

Walk 50 Directions

Harden Beck and Goit Stock Woods are little known, except by locals. If they were situated in the Yorkshire Dales, for example, you would see walkers aplenty. As it is the woods are hidden away, between a trio of unassuming little villages, Harden, Wilsden and Cullingworth. No matter as this is as pleasant a woodland walk as can be found, and all the better for being a little off the beaten track.

Harden Beck runs from Hewenden Reservoir, through Goit Stock Woods and takes a meandering route to join the River Aire close to Beckfoot Bridge near Bingley, a picturesque packhorse bridge encountered on Walk 28. It is only a short walk along Harden Beck to find Goit Stock Falls, which plunge more than 20ft (6m) over a rocky ledge into a pool. While it's no Niagara, it can still be an impressive sight after rain.

These deciduous woods are a little oasis for birds; look out for woodpeckers, jays, treecreepers and – in summer – many species of warbler and other songbirds.

WHAT TO LOOK FOR ⓘ

No one would pretend that West Yorkshire is a rural idyll, since much of the country is uncompromisingly urban. But one unexpected pleasure is to find so much broadleaved woodland. In more celebrated landscapes (the Lake District and North York Moors spring to mind) too much ancient woodland has been supplanted by the serried ranks of conifer trees, which offer little to walkers or wildlife. Goit Stock is one of many delightful and deciduous woods that make welcome green oases in the metropolitan county, supporting a great variety of animals, birds and plants.

Walk 50

As with the waterfall, the drumming of a woodpecker is usually heard long before you get a glimpse of it. If you're lucky you may spot a dipper along the side of the beck.

Walk downhill, turning right just before the bridge, on to **Goit Stock Lane**. Pass a few houses, then a cattle grid, to follow a metalled track alongside **Harden Beck**. Cross the beck, skirt a caravan park and continue on a path beyond the caravanners' car park, signed to the waterfall. Pass a bungalow and enter **Goit Stock Wood**, now with the beck on your right. You have easy walking, as the beck runs through an increasingly steep and rocky gorge. Your progress is halted at **Goit Stock Falls**, which cascades over a rocky ledge into a pool below. Hand-rails on the left help you to scramble up to the top of the waterfall and continue to follow **Harden Beck**, past another, smaller waterfall. A rocky path soon leads to **Hallas Bridge**.

Don't cross the footbridge, but bear acute left, uphill, signed as a bridleway. Keep left of a row of terraced houses, to locate a gap stile in the wall ahead. Follow a field path, skirting woodland on your left. The path takes you over three more stiles; at the fourth stile you re-enter the woods. Pass between

the legs of an electricity pylon. Follow the obvious path through woodland, with a steep slope on your left. Leave the wood via a stile, and follow a field path to meet **Wilsden Road** again. Turn left, and walk down the road. At the end of a garden centre car park take a narrow lane on the left, which takes you steeply down to the **Malt Shovel Inn** and your car.

Walking in Safety

All these walks are suitable for any reasonably fit person, but less experienced walkers should try the easier walks first. Route finding is usually straightforward, but you will find that an Ordnance Survey map is a useful addition to the route maps and descriptions.

Risks

Although each walk here has been researched with a view to minimising the risks to the walkers who follow its route, no walk in the countryside can be considered to be completely free from risk. Walking in the outdoors will always require a degree of common sense and judgement to ensure that it is as safe as possible.

- Be particularly careful on cliff paths and in upland terrain, where the consequences of a slip can be very serious.

- Remember to check tidal conditions before walking on the seashore.

- Some sections of route are by, or cross, busy roads. Take care and remember traffic is a danger even on minor country lanes.

- Be careful around farmyard machinery and livestock, especially if you have children with you.

- Be aware of the consequences of changes in the weather and check the forecast before you set out. Carry spare clothing and a torch if you are walking in the winter months. Remember the weather can change very quickly at any time of the year, and in moorland and heathland areas, mist and fog can make route finding much harder. Don't set out in these conditions unless you are confident of your navigation skills in poor visibility. In summer remember to take account of the heat and sun; wear a hat and carry spare water.

- On walks away from centres of population you should carry a whistle and survival bag. If you do have an accident requiring the emergency services, make a note of your position as accurately as possible and dial 999.

Acknowledgements

From the author
Thanks to the West Yorkshire branch of the Ramblers Association, and everyone in the tourism departments of the five boroughs that make up West Yorkshire: Leeds, Bradford, Wakefield, Kirklees and Calderdale… with a special tip of the hat to Ed Westbrook.

Series management: Outcrop Publishing Services, Cumbria
Series editor: Chris Bagshaw
Front cover: AA Photo Library/R Eames